HIKING MAINE'S
BAXTER STATE PARK

HELP US KEEP THIS GUIDE UP-TO-DATE

Every effort has been made by the author and editors to make this guide as accurate and useful as possible. However, many things may change after a guide is published—trails may be rerouted, regulations may change, techniques may evolve, facilities may come under new management, etc.

We would appreciate hearing from you concerning your experiences with this guide and how you feel it can be improved and kept up-to-date. While we may not be able to respond to all comments and suggestions, we'll take them to heart, and we'll also make certain to share them with the authors. Please send your comments and suggestions to the following address:

Globe Pequot
Reader Response/Editorial Department
246 Goose Lane
Guilford, CT 06437

Or you may e-mail us at: editorial@falcon.com

Thanks for your input, and happy trails!

HIKING MAINE'S
BAXTER STATE PARK

A GUIDE TO THE PARK'S GREATEST HIKING ADVENTURES
INCLUDING MOUNT KATAHDIN

Greg Westrich

GUILFORD, CONNECTICUT

I wish to remember the words and vision of Percival Baxter. Many have followed in Baxter's footsteps and carried his vision forward, protecting and stewarding Katahdin and Baxter State Park. We owe them our gratitude. In the words of Baxter himself:

Katahdin stands above the surrounding plain unique in grandeur and glory. The works of man are short-lived. Monuments decay, buildings crumble, and wealth vanishes, but Katahdin in its massive grandeur will forever remain the mountain of the people of Maine.

FALCONGUIDES®

An imprint of Globe Pequot
Falcon and FalconGuides are registered trademarks and Make Adventure Your Story is a trademark of Rowman & Littlefield.

Distributed by NATIONAL BOOK NETWORK

Copyright © 2017 Rowman & Littlefield
Photos by Greg Westrich
TOPO! Maps copyright 2017 National Geographic Partners, LLC. All Rights Reserved.
Maps © Rowman & Littlefield

British Library Cataloguing-in-Publication Information available

Library of Congress Cataloging-in-Publication Data available

ISBN 978-1-4930-1900-7 (paperback)
ISBN 978-1-4930-1901-4 (e-book)

∞™ The paper used in this publication meets the minimum requirements of American National Standard for Information Sciences—Permanence of Paper for Printed Library Materials, ANSI/NISO Z39.48-1992.

Printed in the United States of America

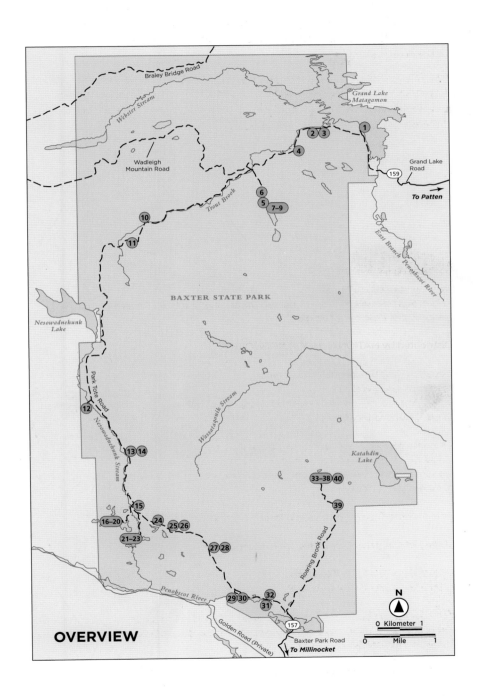

Braley Bridge Road

Webster Stream

Grand Lake
Matagamon

Wadleigh
Mountain Road

(2) (3)   (1)

(4)

Grand Lake
Road

159

To Patten

Trout Brook

(6)
(5) (7–9)

East Branch Penobscot River

(10)

(11)

BAXTER STATE PARK

Nesowadnehunk
Lake

Park Tote Road

(12)

Nesowadnehunk Stream

Wassataquoik Stream

Katahdin
Lake

(13)(14)

(33–38)(40)

(39)

(15)

(16–20)   (24)
           (25)(26)

(21–23)

(27)(28)

Roaring Brook Road

(29)(30)   (32)
           (31)

Penobscot River

Golden Road (Private)

157

Baxter Park Road
To Millinocket

N

0 Kilometer 1
0   Mile   1

OVERVIEW

Descending North Traveler.
The South Branch Ponds
are just visible.

THE HIKES

MEET YOUR GUIDE

When I was eight, my parents took me and my two younger brothers on our first camping trip in a borrowed tent. It rained the whole weekend. What I remember most about the trip was standing in a light mist beneath drooping white pines on Sunday morning. A great horned owl dropped from a nearby tree and floated silently between the rusty trunks and out of sight. It was childhood moments of wonder and awe seeing that owl that lit my hiking bug.

By the time I graduated from college, I'd visited every state but Hawaii and most of Canada. I settled with my wife in Maine, where we've lived for 20 years. We hike, camp, canoe, ski, and generally love our wild home. Seven years ago, I quit my day job to hike and write full time.

I have backpacked from one end of Baxter State Park to the other, climbed Katahdin eight times, and hiked more than 200 of the 215 miles of trails in the park. In the last 2 years alone, I've hiked almost 400 miles in Baxter.

I'm the author of four previous FalconGuides, and am currently working on several others. Since 2013, I've mapped more than 500 hikes in Maine. I've also published more than fifty articles and stories in newspapers, anthologies, and magazines, including *Canoe & Kayak, Bird Watching,* and *Down East.* I have an MFA in creative writing from the University of Southern Maine's Stonecoast Program, and I teach writing at Husson University and Eastern Maine Community College. I live in Glenburn with my family and too many pets. You can follow my hiking life on Facebook or gregwestrich.com.

HOW TO USE THIS GUIDE

The day hikes in this guide are listed from north to south. There's a separate section for backpacking trips. You can create an almost infinite number of trips in Baxter. This guide only includes a few that reach destinations not accessible by day hikes.

After a brief overview of each hike, you'll find the quick, nitty-gritty details: where the trailhead is located, elevation gain, total hike length, approximate hiking time, difficulty rating, best hiking season, type of trail terrain, nearest town, other trail users you may encounter, water sources, and maps. The "Finding the Trailhead" section gives you dependable directions from either the Matagamon or Togue Pond Gate right to where you'll want to park your car. The "What to See" section is the meat of the chapter, where you'll get a more detailed description of the trail. In "Miles and Directions" section, mileage cues identify all turns and trail name changes, as well as points of interest. Many of the hikes have reliable water sources, but except for the few springs all water should be treated before drinking.

Map Legends

Each hike begins with **The Rundown**, a summary that describes the length of the trip and the basic geography. For day hikes, most entries indicate the approximate time required for the hike, using these three categories as general rules of thumb, based on an average adult hiking pace and decent trail conditions: "Short day hikes" are, generally, hikes of 3 hours or less; "half-day hikes" take roughly 3 to 5 hours; and "long hikes" will keep you outdoors more than 5 hours and up to an entire sunset-free day in midsummer. There are options for shorter hikes on most of the longer trips covered; options are listed in "Shorter hikes" at the end of the narrative.

Distances shown are the actual distance of the trail or route. For traverses or loops, this is the entire distance of the trip. Distances shown as "one way" indicate out-and-back hikes; if you do the entire round-trip, you'll cover double the listed trail mileage.

Difficulty ratings give a general sense of how strenuous a hike is. The ratings correspond to elevation gain, tempered by the grade, length, and hiking surface.

Easy: can be completed without difficulty by hikers of all abilities
Moderate: is challenging for novices
Strenuous: may tax even experienced hikers
Very strenuous: difficult even for experienced hikers

Trail type refers to the degree of development of the trail. Accessible trails are packed and graded and suitable for mobility-impaired people, including those who use wheelchairs. "More-developed" trails are planned and constructed trails with some combination of trail structures like bridges or foot logs over streams, switchbacks, steps, bench-cut tread on side slopes, boardwalk in wet areas, signs, and for the most part, a clear path and relatively even tread.

"Less-developed" trails may in places have structures like more-developed trails, but they are generally rougher and will take longer to hike. While there is a tread to follow in most places, it may be only the tread other hikers have made with their boot soles. Less-developed trails are usually maintained less frequently. They are common in Alaska's state parks.

A "route" may be marked with rock cairns, wooden posts, or fiberglass stakes and follow intermittent sections of tread laid down by hikers' feet, but is rough and may be difficult to follow in places. "Cross-country" refers to travel following a line of geography like a stream or ridgeline without any marking or tread to follow. "Path" as used here refers to any tread hikers can follow on the ground.

Total elevation gain is a figure in vertical feet that reflects all the uphill grade on the hike; if there are significant ups and downs, the figure includes a rough total of all the "ups," so in many cases it's more than the elevation of the destination minus the elevation of the trailhead.

HOW TO USE THE PROFILES AND MAPS

This book uses elevation profiles to provide an idea of the elevation changes you will encounter along each route. This, in turn, will help you understand the difficulty of the hike. In the profiles, the vertical axes of the graphs show the total distance climbed in feet. In contrast, the horizontal axes show the distance traveled one way in miles. It is important to understand that the vertical (feet) and horizontal (miles) scales can differ between hikes. Read each profile carefully, making sure you read both the height and distance shown. This will help you interpret what you see in each profile. Some elevation profiles may show gradual ascents and descents to be steep and steep ones to be gradual. Elevation profiles are not provided for hikes with little or no elevation gain.

The maps in this book that depict a detailed close-up of an area use color to portray relief. These maps will give you a good idea of elevation gain and loss. They are a good reference, but should not replace USGS Topographic Maps that should be used as the navigational tool.

ABOUT THE MAPS

Topographic maps are an essential companion to the activities in this guide. Falcon has partnered with National Geographic to provide the best mapping resources. Each activity is accompanied by a detailed map and the name of the National Geographic TOPO! map (USGS).

If the activity takes place on a National Geographic Trails Illustrated map, it will be noted. Continually setting the standard for accuracy, each Trails Illustrated topographic map is crafted in conjunction with local land managers and undergoes rigorous review and enhancement before being printed on waterproof, tear-resistant material. Trails Illustrated maps and information about their digital versions, that can be used on mobile GPS applications, can be found at natgeomaps.com.

MAP LEGEND

▪▪▪▪▪▪	Featured Route on Trail
- - - - -	Trail
—(157)—	State Road
———	County/Other/FR
– – –	Gravel Road
🚌	Bench
‿	Bridge
‖‖‖‖‖	Boardwalk/Steps
⚠	Campground
•—•	Gate
P	Parking
▲	Peak
⚏	Picnic Area
☐	Point of Interest
🛈	Ranger Station/Park Office
🚻	Restroom
🔭	Scenic View
🔍	Spring
①	Trailhead
?	Visitor/Information Center
🗾	Waterfall
～	River/Stream/Brook
⬭	Lake
⸰⸰⸰	Marsh/Bog

Chimney Pond in Great Basin.

BEFORE YOU HIT THE TRAIL

In 1804, Charles Turner made the first recorded ascent of Katahdin. He'd been commissioned by Massachusetts—Maine was part of Massachusetts until 1820—to survey Maine. His party climbed Katahdin by following Katahdin Stream from the West Branch Penobscot River to where Katahdin Stream Campground is today. From there, they ascended the Hunt Spur, the same route as today's Hunt Trail. Turner estimated that Katahdin was 13,000 feet high.

In the 30 years that followed, Katahdin was climbed several more times by surveying or scientific parties. It wasn't until 1845 that Katahdin was climbed recreationally. (For comparison, Mount Washington in New Hampshire's White Mountains was first climbed in 1642 by Darby Field to impress the local Indians on behalf of the Massachusetts government.) Edward Hale and William Channing—acquaintances of Henry David Thoreau and fellow Harvard graduates—climbed Katahdin from the north. They were turned back by weather somewhere on the North Peaks. Theirs was the first ascent from the north.

But I'm getting ahead of the story. As the last of the glacial cover melted, 12,000 years ago, life returned to the Katahdin region. Paleo-Indians followed the animals up the valleys between glacier-carved mountains. Their ancestors still live in Maine. It's their names and lore that introduced whites to Katahdin and its surroundings. The Penobscots hunted and fished in what today is Baxter State Park. They'd no need to climb the mountains. Besides, the storm god Pamola lived on Katahdin. He influenced the weather and was said to eat anyone who tried to ascend his mountain. Given the way Katahdin makes its own weather—a cloud is almost always swirling around the summit—it's no surprise that the Penobscots would have passed down stories to explain why. Even though they never climbed the mountain, Penobscots were instrumental in guiding whites to the base of the mountain. To this day, Katahdin holds a special place in the spiritual lives of the region's Indians.

Pamola is known today mostly through the tales of Leroy Dudley. Dudley built the first cabin at Chimney Pond in 1924. He spent his summers there guiding tourists up and around Katahdin until the 1940s. In the evenings, he regaled the "sports" with tales. One of his favorite subjects was Pamola, who he claimed to have befriended. In the 1930s, Clayton Hall so enjoyed Dudley's tales that he lugged an office-dictating machine into Chimney Pond and recorded the stories. Much later, Hall's niece and Jane Thomas—who had heard Dudley as a youngster—found Hall's manuscript and published it.

Evidently, Dudley came by his Pamola lore naturally. He was part Penobscot, probably related to the Neptune family. The short, brutally steep trail from Chimney Pond to Pamola Peak—passing the caves where Pamola lives—bears his name. It's one of several trails Dudley built in his years on the mountain.

Everyone has at least one good Katahdin story. After all, you can see the mountain from as far away as Orono. Thoreau commented that he first saw the mountain from the stage as it crossed Bangor Hill. Today, especially in winter, you can see Katahdin from northbound I-95 just south of the Old Town exit.

Katahdin and the wilderness surrounding it pulls many Mainers and folks from away. We are drawn to it like moths to a porch light. Many people who aren't peak baggers or even hikers feel the need to climb Katahdin at least once. Appalachian Trail (AT) thru-hikers begin looking for Katahdin on the horizon almost as soon as they enter Maine.

LOST ON A MOUNTAIN IN MAINE

Probably the most famous Katahdin story is that of Donn Fendler. Twelve-year-old Fendler climbed Katahdin on July 17, 1939, with a group from Rye, New York. In swirling clouds on the cold summit, he became confused and descended the wrong way—he hiked down into The Saddle rather than returning down Hunt Trail. In The Saddle, he headed west, descending into The Klondike. He wandered lost for nine days. A massive manhunt was organized. It became national front-page news. Searchers never found Fendler. Instead, the boy followed Wassataquoik Stream and found his own way out. During his ordeal, he'd no food except what he found in the woods, no shelter, and was beset by biting insects. He crossed rough terrain and suffered through summer storms. When he emerged near Staceyville, his clothes were in tatters and he'd lost 16 pounds. He credited his Boy Scout training with getting him through it all.

Fendler's story was turned into a book by Joseph B. Egan. Almost every school kid in Maine has read the book. Many have met Fendler who still makes regular appearances at schools to share his story.

THE GEOLOGY OF BAXTER STATE PARK

Long before Donn Fendler got lost on a mountain in Maine, before Henry David Thoreau climbed to Katahdin's Table Land, before the first timber cruiser paddled down Webster Stream and across Grand Lake Matagamon, and even before the Penobscots' ancestors felt the pull of the mountain they named Katahdin, the region that became Baxter State Park had stories to tell. Those stories are written in rock.

Baxter State Park has a complex geological history. The mountains and ponds we see today were shaped by glaciers. Most people know that Katahdin's many basins were carved by glaciers grinding away the mountain's bedrock. Glaciation created many of the park's ponds, too. At least three different processes were at work to make the ponds. First, many kettle ponds were created by huge chunks of ice that sat melting as the glaciers retreated. The ice formed depressions in the ground that filled with water as the ice disappeared. Many of the ponds along the park's southern edge are kettle ponds.

Second, most basins in the park have a tarn. These ponds are often very picturesque. Chimney Pond, Davis Pond, and Twin Pond are all tarns nestled in basins. Finally, glaciers grind up bedrock and push it around. As a glacier advances, a huge pile of rubble collects at its toe. When the glacier retreats, this rubble forms a dam-like hill called a moraine. Often ponds form behind moraines before the streams find a way through or around the dam. The Basin Ponds at the mouth of Great Basin are such ponds.

The glaciers are also responsible for the U-shaped valleys and almost vertical mountainsides in the park. The bedrock on these slopes was cleared of soil and polished smooth. After the glaciers retreated, a layer of debris was left covering everything. But the layer of debris and new soil has a hard time adhering to the steep slopes and smooth bedrock. As a result, many of Baxter's mountains have huge slides and areas of exposed bedrock on their flanks.

In addition to piling ground rock and debris into moraines, glaciers push debris along their flanks. When the glaciers retreat, an esker is left behind—a long, narrow hill of debris. Eskers are found throughout the park and around Maine. Road and trails are often built atop them—a good way to cross swampy lowlands. They're often mined for sand and gravel. The park's Tote Road crosses an esker between Togue Pond Gate and Abol Beach Road. Several trails in the park follow eskers above bogs and ponds. Eskers and kettle ponds are often found together in Baxter.

The mountains of Baxter State Park were formed millions of years before the glaciers most recently shaped them. Katahdin is part of a huge granite pluton that formed about 400 million years ago during what geologists call the Acadian orogeny. At that time, the North American and European plates collided. The violence of the collision was such that when the Atlantic Ocean opened up millions of years later, the European plate was ripped apart—part of it remained attached to North America. Nova Scotia and the coast of Maine are geologically related to Greenland, Iceland, and Scotland, not the rest of North America.

This geological violence led to the creation of Maine's granite plutons. Granite is formed deep within the Earth when molten rock cools and crystallizes. Generally, the rock is only exposed when the overlying layers erode away. It's believed that Katahdin formed about 9 miles below the surface. Then over the following millions

Granite outcropping

of years, much of the granite became exposed. The pluton that includes Katahdin extends from North Turner Mountain southwest almost as far as Greenville. Katahdin is like the tip of this giant rock iceberg. As you hike around Baxter, you'll notice that all the granite isn't the same. It varies in color, texture, and erosivity. In general, the hardest and pinkest granite is found atop the highest mountains. This granite atop the pluton cooled into glass originally. It acts as a hard cap on the mountains, slowing erosion. Take time to notice the variability of the rock: for example, between Pamola and Baxter Peaks or between the base of North Brother and its summit.

Granite tends to be rough and offers good footing for hiking and climbing. Erosion breaks it into angular boulders along fracture lines. The boulders eventually break into their constituent crystals, creating rough sand. The bed of many streams in southern Baxter and the beaches on Togue Pond and Katahdin Lake are ground granite.

About the same time Katahdin's granite was created, a huge volcano erupted to the north. The eruption covered a huge area with thick ash and outflow—think Mount St. Helens but bigger. This volcanic rock became the rhyolite bedrock that makes up the mountains in northern Baxter. The Traveler is the largest of the rhyolite mountains that extend from South Pogy Mountain northeast to Horse Mountain.

Rhyolite looks a lot like granite and is made of many of the same components. It often forms hexagonal columns. You can see evidence of this on the Little Knife Edge and low on North Traveler where the trail first breaks out of the woods. Rhyolite's different origin makes it weather differently from granite. On mountain tops, it tends to fracture into many smaller components. Small bits of broken rock cover the bedrock, making footing difficult. Descending off North Traveler is a very different experience from descending Katahdin.

North of these mountains, the bedrock is much younger sedimentary rock. Where the waterfalls in central and southern Baxter are over granite bedrock, those in the north are over slate—geologically related to the many waterfalls in the Central Highlands, not the others in Baxter. Along Trout Brook and Webster Stream, you can find a sedimentary conglomerate rock. It looks superficially like the glacial debris that fills the valleys in the southern part of the park, but is of different origin.

Mount Chase and Sugarloaf Mountain across the East Branch from Baxter may look like the mountains of northern Baxter, but they're geologically unrelated. Where almost all the mountains in Baxter are made of igneous rock created during the Acadian orogeny, those mountains that dot the North Woods are mainly sedimentary rock. Sugarloaf even has fossils in its bedrock. This includes those in Katahdin Woods and Waters National Monument such as Deasey and Bernard Mountains.

BUILDING BAXTER STATE PARK

The year Dudley built his cabin on Chimney Pond, Percival Baxter was finishing his term as Maine's governor. He'd repeatedly—as governor and before that as a state legislator—tried to get the state to buy Katahdin and make it a state park. The entrenched interests of the timber companies and landholding families were too strong. After leaving government in 1925, Baxter decided to use his wealth to buy the mountain himself for the people of Maine.

His attachment to Katahdin began in 1903 when he stayed at Kidney Pond with his father on a fishing trip. The commercial camps at Kidney and Daicey Ponds had been in operation for a few years. They were becoming increasingly popular. Baxter didn't climb Katahdin on that trip. Not until 1920, when he joined a group of Republican politicians and prominent citizens on the mountain, did he stand atop Maine's highest peak. The group met up in Patten and made their way up Wassataquoik Stream to Katahdin Lake. From there, they trekked to Chimney Pond, guided by Dudley. Part of the group climbed Katahdin via The Saddle—there was no trail, but a recognizable route. Baxter, Dudley, and some others climbed what became

Columns of rhyolite on lower North Traveler Mountain

Pamola Peak and the Knife Edge across Great Basin from Baxter Peak

Dudley Trail to Pamola Peak and across the Knife Edge. Baxter was so awed by the experience that he decided to try and protect the mountain for the people of Maine.

In November 1930, Baxter bought Katahdin and about 6,000 acres around it for $25,000. In 1933, the state formally accepted his gift and renamed Katahdin's highest peak—then known as Monument Peak—Baxter Peak. Baxter continued buying land and donating it to the park. In 1962, he made his twenty-eighth and final donation. The park had grown to 200,000 acres.

What makes Baxter State Park so unique is the way Baxter donated the land. Each parcel was transferred with a deed that specified how the land could be used. Baxter wanted the park preserved as a wilderness. Many of the park's rules—such as its prohibition on dogs—are written into the deeds. The park was also endowed and is run by a committee of state officials. Baxter State Park isn't part of the state's park system. The primary job of the Baxter State Park Authority is to preserve the "resource." That is to ensure that the woods, ponds, and mountains remain forever wild. Recreation is of lesser concern. All of this is in the deeds.

In the late 1930s, there was a move to make Baxter State Park a national park. Baxter opposed. He wanted the park to remain free for the people of Maine and free of the typical national park development. To this day, Baxter State Park has no electricity, no running water, no plumbing, no phone service, and doesn't allow pets or motor homes or motorcycles. There are no garbage cans, no paved roads, and no cell phone service. Even the rangers living in the park do without these everyday amenities.

They communicate by radio, bathe in ponds, and get their only electricity from a handful of solar panels. Their light is from propane lanterns. Under the watchful eye of Baxter, and now the Baxter State Park Authority, some of the most intensively logged land in Maine has become the Eastern United States greatest wilderness.

Since Baxter's death in 1969, Baxter State Park has been expanded. The area between the southern border of the park and the West Branch was added, including the Togue Ponds. In 2006, in a complex land deal that involved the state government, logging companies, and several nonprofits, Katahdin Lake was added to the park. Baxter himself always regretted that he'd been unable to buy the land around Katahdin Lake. It seems unlikely that any more land will be added to the 209,644 acres.

In the early years of the park, the Civilian Conservation Corps was instrumental in building and maintaining many of the park's facilities, including the Tote Road. The Tote Road is a 46-mile-long gravel road that runs from Togue Pond Gate, west to the Nesowadnehunk Valley, then north along the western edge of the park. Finally, the road cuts east to Matagamon Gate in the park's northeast corner. There are shorter gravel roads to the Roaring Brook area, Daicey Pond, Kidney Pond, and Lower South Branch Pond.

GETTING TO BAXTER STATE PARK

Baxter has two entrances. The south entrance is at Togue Pond. To get there, get off I-95 at exit 244. Follow ME 157 through Medway and East Millinocket to Millinocket. Where ME 157 ends, turn right onto Katahdin Avenue. Drive 0.2 mile and turn left onto Bates Street at the park sign. As you leave Millinocket, Bates Street becomes Baxter Road. Follow it all the way to the park's south entrance. It's 39.2 miles from I-95 to Togue Pond Gate. There's lodging and a small store at Ambejejus Lake, but no gas beyond Millinocket.

To get to the north gate, get off I-95 at exit 264. Follow ME 11 north to Patten. In Patten, turn left onto ME 159. At Shin Pond, ME 159 becomes Grand Lake Road. Follow this road all the way into the park. It's 35.8 miles from I-95 to the Matagamon Gate. There's a commercial camp with a store and a restaurant just outside the park along the East Branch Penobscot River. There's also lodging and a small store at Shin Pond. The last gas is in Patten.

Use the appropriate park entrance for each hike. Don't plan to drive from one end of the park to the other on the Tote Road. The speed limit on all park roads is 20 mph—10 mph in busy areas. The roads are narrow and winding, wildlife is abundant, and the views can be distracting. Please obey the speed limit. This means it takes more than 2 hours to drive from Togue Pond Gate to Matagamon Gate.

Visitors not from Maine pay an auto entrance fee at the gate.

STAYING IN BAXTER STATE PARK

The park has nine campgrounds. Two of those, Kidney Pond and Daicey Pond, are former commercial camps where you can rent a cabin. Two more, Russell and

The lean-to at Webster Pond is typical of those in Baxter

Chimney Ponds, are remote campgrounds with lean-tos, tent sites, and a bunkhouse that you have to backpack to. The others, Trout Brook Farm, Lower South Branch Pond, Nesowadnehunk Field, Katahdin Stream, and Abol Stream, have a mix of tent sites and lean-tos with auto access. In addition to the campgrounds, the park has numerous backcountry campsites. Most have four or six person lean-tos, but some are tent sites. Many, like Upper South Branch Pond and Wassataquoik Lake, are very popular. Many of the others go regularly unused.

All campsites have well-maintained pit toilets. All campsites are near a water source. You need to treat all water in the park before drinking or cooking with it. Don't use soap, dish detergent, or toothpaste in the park. Soaps can contaminate water supplies and harm wildlife.

You can make a reservation for any campsite on the park's website (http://www.baxterstateparkauthority.com/) or by calling (207) 723-5140. Reservations can be made up to four months in advance. For popular sites, plan and make your reservations on the first possible day. If you wish to stay at Kidney or Daicey Ponds, call the park in early January. There are special rules for reserving cabins farther ahead.

In addition to park facilities, Katahdin Lake Wilderness Camps is a commercial camp on Katahdin Lake within the park. For more information on this historic camp, visit their website at http://www.katahdinlakewildernesscamps.com.

Outside the park, there are lots of choices from campgrounds to inns to commercial camps. Begin your search at the Katahdin Area Chamber of Commerce's website at http://katahdinmaine.com/lodging.

HIKING IN BAXTER STATE PARK

Many of the mountains in Baxter have exposed summits above tree line. Weather there can be colder and wetter than at the trailhead. I've left Roaring Brook on a

Daicey Pond library and the famous twin pines

sunny day in the 70s and reached Baxter Peak to find a wet wind and the temperature in the 50s. At the same time, Pamola Peak keeps the weather on and around Katahdin unpredictable. Plan accordingly: try not to wear cotton clothing, it gets wet with sweat or rain and chills you; always take a rain gear or a coat; keep extra food and safety equipment in your pack, such as a headlamp, a lighter, and a first-aid kit; and carry plenty of water. In spring and fall, it's a good idea to carry hat and gloves if you are hiking above tree line.

A lot of the hiking in Baxter is very remote. This solitude is wonderful and increases the likelihood you'll encounter wildlife. But it also means there's no one around to help if you get in trouble. Your cell phone can't bail you out. Know your limits and hike accordingly. Be prepared for the weather to worsen. Carry this guidebook or map and know where you are. Be prepared for the worst and enjoy whatever nature and Baxter gives you.

Many of the trails in the park are lightly maintained, but generally well-blazed and easy to follow. Any exceptions are noted in the text for each hike. But remember beavers regularly flood trails and new blowdowns happen all the time. The park asks that you sign in and out for each hike and report any problems you encounter on the trail.

Off-trail hiking is allowed in Baxter. In fact, many scenic areas and mountains in the park are untrailed. This was done intentionally so that those with the woods skills and compass and map abilities can explore real wilderness. If you plan to hike off-trail, consult a ranger about your route and destination. There are established routes on many of the untrailed mountains such as Wassataquoik, Fort, North Turner, and Pogy.

If you are starting your hike from Roaring Brook, Katahdin Stream, or Abol campground, it's best to reserve a day-use parking space. These three trailheads have

Sign near Abol Trailhead

limited parking and are very popular, because they're where the three routes up Katahdin start. You can make a reservation on the park's website (http://www.baxterstateparkauthority.com/) or by calling (207) 723-5140. There's a small fee. **The reservation will only be held until 7:05 a.m.**

WILDLIFE

Maine has the greatest concentration of bears of any state, but you are unlikely to see one on a hike. It may be because there's so much habitat for them to roam around in, or because bears are widely hunted in the state. Still, reasonable precaution should be taken, especially with food. Maybe you'll get lucky and see one at a distance. In two dozen trips to Baxter, I've seen exactly one bear.

Many people come to Maine to look for moose; they're rarely disappointed. You are much more likely to see a moose than a bear while hiking. The best places to see them are where their food is. In the summer, look where there's aquatic vegetation. In spring and fall, look where there's a good hardwood browse. In winter, they tend to congregate on south-facing slopes with hardwoods near stands of thick softwoods. But moose do move around—especially bulls—and can be found almost anywhere, even high on rocky mountains. Moose are big animals and find it easier to travel on roads and trails than in thick woods, so be sure to look around as you drive. The best places to see moose are noted in each hike.

Maine is home to coyotes. Not the small western ones that skulk about, but wolf-like coyotes that hunt deer. They're fairly common, but you are unlikely to see one of these beautiful animals. At night, though, you may be serenaded by their spine-tingling howls, especially in the northern part of the park.

Maine is home to numerous weasels and rodents. You are unlikely to see one of the weasels, but it's quite a treat when you see a stoat, a fisher, or an otter. If you hear a group of blue jays making a racket in the tree tops, check it out: They are probably mobbing an egg and chick predator such as a fisher, eagle, or hawk.

You would be hard pressed to take a hike free of squirrels. They sit on downfalls or in trees, commenting loudly on passing hikers. Beavers are common in Baxter's lakes and streams. Their handiwork is easy to

Cow moose and her calf in a beaver pond with Horse Mountain in the background

Snowshoe hare on Celia & Jackson Ponds Trail

find, but seeing one of the shy rodents is less common. They're most active in the twilight of early morning and late evening. The best places to find them and their dams are noted in each hike's text.

By weight, there are more salamanders in Maine than moose. Which is another way to say that most wildlife isn't big but small. You may not see a bear or a moose on a hike, but you'll—if you look around you—see plenty of wildlife. A dozen of species of amphibians are out there for you to find. It isn't uncommon to see several kinds of frogs and toads on a hike. Maine also has several kinds of snakes—none poisonous—that often sun on warm trails.

Maine is a magnet for birders because of the diverse habitats and the presence of northern species not found elsewhere in the United States. Their songs are a constant presence on hikes, whether it's the chatter of a family of chickadees, the musical song of a hermit thrush, or the eerie wail of a loon. Your ears will find many more birds than your eyes. On Katahdin, you can find American pipits—a small, inconspicuous bird that nests on the ground. The Table Land is one of the only places east of the Mississippi, where they breed in the United States. Generally, they're found in the Arctic tundra.

BUGS

One theory holds that Maine is so sparsely populated because of the biting insects. They can be quite annoying—even ruin an otherwise great day of hiking. There

American toad sitting on North Basin Trail

are black flies, checker flies, moose flies, no-see-ums, and mosquitoes. Black flies are worst between Mother's Day and Father's Day, but are around all summer, especially at elevation. They're only active during the day. Black flies' saliva numbs your skin, so you often aren't aware of all your bites until they start itching the next day. Over time, their bites seem to cause less swelling and itching, as if the immune system learns to fight back. Even so, when they're at their worst, many Mainers wear a bug net over their head for protection. When they're at their worst, try to remember that they're an important food for trout and a primary pollinator for wild blueberries.

Mosquitoes are active day and night, and are most common in cool, damp areas. Which means that unless there's snow on the ground, there's something out there wanting to bite you. In general, late spring is the worst season for bugs. The buggiest place in all of Baxter is the Togue Pond Gate. You can judge how the bugs will be elsewhere by opening your car windows while you wait your turn to enter the park.

Ticks have become a problem in Maine over the last several years. I've pulled hundreds of ticks off myself during and after hikes, but I've never gotten a tick in Baxter. They're around, just not as common as in warmer parts of the state. Always check your shoes, pants, and legs after each hike, especially after walking through tall grass.

Always carry bug dope. Having said that, you'll have many bug-free hiking days, especially when it's breezy.

Lady slipper orchid in bloom along a trail

PLANT LIFE

Tourists flock to New England in the fall for the foliage, and it's well worth the trip, but what many people—even native Mainers—miss are the spring colors. When the trees begin to leaf out, the mountainsides are awash in varying shades of green with reds and yellows thrown in. Maybe it's not as dramatic as in the fall, but beautiful just the same. Beneath the trees, a profusion of wildflowers rush to bloom before the canopy closes and leaves them in the shade for the summer.

Through the summer, a succession of berries ripen for hikers to snack on. Especially prized are blueberries. In this guide, good blueberry spots are noted. The blueberries usually begin to ripen in late July.

In the fall, beneath the vibrant trees, there's an explosion of mushrooms. There are at least a thousand varieties of fungi native to Maine. Most of the time they live

Round-leaf sundew

unobserved within the soil, in rotting vegetation, and on tree roots. But in the fall they bloom: Fungi send up fruiting bodies that release spores—like tiny seeds—into the air. We call these fruiting bodies mushrooms.

Baxter's bogs and wetlands are home to a variety of interesting plants, including several carnivorous species. The best places to find these plant oddities are noted in the text.

WINTER

Most of Baxter's facilities are closed from late October until May. Mountain trails close as soon as the snow begins to fall. Grand Lake Road is plowed as far as Matagamon Wilderness Campground & Cabins, making access from the north difficult. You can ski in or use a snowmobile—they're allowed on the Tote Road.

On the south side, Baxter Road is plowed as far as Ambejejus Lake, 8 miles from the Togue Pond Gate. The park recommends you access the southern part of the park from Abol Bridge, which is only a half mile from the Baxter boundary. The park has a winter use map on its website (http://www.baxterstateparkauthority .com/maps/winter.htm). Remember that none of the trails are groomed. You need a special permit for all-winter hiking in the park.

Baxter in the winter is a spectacular and challenging place. But if you have the skills and proper equipment, a winter trip can be immensely rewarding.

SPRING

The last of the snow doesn't melt off the high peaks in Baxter until June or even July. Because so much of the precipitation in Baxter is snow, stream levels are very high in the spring. As you hike around the park, it may occur to you how few stream crossings are bridged. This is not only to maintain the Baxter's wilderness character, but also because most would just wash away with the spring freshet. When you visit the park before June, check to see what water levels are like on your route. Some stream crossings can be dangerous during high water, such as those on Wassataquoik Stream. Remember, too, that boggy and marshy areas are wetter in spring, and often flood trails and mountain trails turn to streams. Don't let the wet dissuade you from hiking, just be prepared.

SUMMER

Weekends in the summer can be busy in Baxter. But even on the finest days, you can still find solitude on most hikes. On any given summer day, about half the people hiking in Baxter are on Katahdin. The summit can be crowded with fifty people. Thru-hikers are completing or beginning the AT adventure. Day hikers are gawking at Chimney Pond 2,000 feet below or at the endless expanse of the North Woods. Friends and family members are congratulating each other for making it across the Knife Edge or up Abol Trail. It's certainly an experience we all need to have. This guide offers three different ways to reach Baxter Peak. But don't limit yourself to Katahdin's highest peaks. There are more than 200 miles of trails in Baxter and they're all worth hiking. Most of them you can have all to yourself. Well, you and the loons and moose.

FALL

September can be a great time to visit Baxter. After the first frost, the bugs are gone. Once school starts, the crowds are gone, too. Nights are cool—even cold—the days warm. The leaves change, valleys and mountainsides explode with red and yellow. Not just the trees change color: blueberries and other bushes turn flame red; ferns go yellow, then almost purple. The very light seems to change color.

Weather in the fall can be unpredictable and changeable. It can snow on the mountains any time. I once left South Branch Pond on a warm, sunny day in October only to be caught in freezing rain and strong wind on North Traveler.

IMPORTANT THINGS TO REMEMBER WHEN YOU VISIT BAXTER STATE PARK

- No dogs or other pets are allowed in the park.
- The only available sources of water in the park are streams, ponds, and springs. All water should be treated before drinking.
- There's no cell service or electricity in the park.
- Visitors not from Maine need to pay an auto entrance fee.

Sign at a junction on Russell Pond Trail

You never know what you'll find

- Motorcycles and motor homes aren't allowed in the park. See the park's website for more specific vehicle restrictions.
- There are no services in the park. Fill your gas tank before leaving either Patton or Millinocket. Bring everything else you'll need for your visit.
- There are no garbage cans in the park. Pack out everything you bring in.
- Rangers and other park employees are knowledgeable and helpful. Talk to them.
- You aren't allowed to bring firewood into the park. Wood can be purchased at ranger's stations or collected in the woods.
- You aren't allowed to use detergents or soap in the park.
- You are welcome to bring your kayak or canoe to the park. The park supplies paddles and PFDs for their rental canoes.
- Obey all park rules. The rules protect Baxter and you.

The Mount O-J-I Trail just below Old Jay Eye Rock

DAY HIKES

A hiker leans into a steep section
of South Branch Mountain Trail

SHOES

In 2001, Susan and Lucy Letcher, sisters from Maine, thru-hiked the Appalachian Trail. Barefoot. When they finished their southbound hike in Georgia, they turned around and walked home. Barefoot, again. They actually wore shoes when there was snow on the ground, but hiked thousands of miles barefoot. Susan and Lucy claimed it wasn't painful and that they tripped less often than booted thru-hikers. They felt much more connected to the trail and the world. Since reading their two books about their AT adventure, I've seen several barefoot hikers in Maine. They seemed comfortable enough, but I still haven't tried it.

I recommend shoes. But what shoes should you wear to hike? There are hiking boots, light hikers, trail runners, some with Gortex, some all leather, and some with Vibram soles. Conventional wisdom says you should wear hiking boots for backpacking and at least light hiking boots for day hiking. Boots, the argument goes, are waterproof and offer better support for ankles and soles.

That may be true, but I haven't worn boots in years. I wear running shoes, even for backpacking. It's true that running shoes in the rain and on some of Baxter's wetter trails didn't really work for my feet. It's also true that after a day of pounding granite my feet ache. The reason I stick with shoes over boots is simple: weight. Heavy boots make me do more work with each step and lead to knee pain and muscle fatigue.

Greg's hiking shoes for 2016

1. HORSE MOUNTAIN

WHY GO?

Horse Mountain Cliffs are the first thing visitors to the north entrance of Baxter see as they approach the park. The Horse Mountain Trail leads to the top of the cliffs with fine views. A side trail leads to the mountain's wooded summit. The main trail continues across the mountain to Billfish Pond. A side trail leads steeply down to Billfish Brook, where it enters a narrow gorge.

THE RUN DOWN

Start: From the Horse Mountain Trailhead at the south end of the parking area.

Elevation gain: 805 feet.

Distance: 3.0 miles out and back.

Hiking time: About 2 hours.

Difficulty: Moderate.

Seasons: May–Oct are best.

Trail surface: Woodland path.

Nearest town: Patten.

Other users: None.

Water availability: None.

Other maps: *DeLorme's The Maine Atlas and Gazetteer* map 51.

Nat Geo TOPO! Map (USGS): Trout Brook Mountain.

Nat Geo Trails Illustrated Map: Baxter State Park.

FINDING THE TRAILHEAD

From the Matagamon Gate, drive 0.7 mile. The trailhead and parking area on the left.
Trailhead GPS: N46° 09.568' / W68° 48.868'.

WHAT TO SEE

The first thing you notice as you approach the north entrance to Baxter is the Horse Mountain Cliffs. The rough, irregular dome of bedrock looms over Grand Lake Matagamon. A scree slope of broken boulders slides down from the base of the cliffs into the hardwoods.

Horse Mountain is the northernmost of a group of mountains built of rhyolite—a crumbly volcanic rock that superficially resembles granite. These mountains are remnants of an eruption so ancient that no other evidence of it remains.

Looking toward The Traveler from East Lookout

The trailhead is on the north side of the mountain where the Tote Road crosses Horse Mountain's shoulder. The Horse Mountain Trail climbs steadily through hardwoods to the undulating summit ridge. The first side trail lead east to the cliff tops, where you have expansive views across Grand Lake Matagamon of the North Woods.

Another side trail leads west up an easy climb to Horse Mountain's wooded summit. The Horse Mountain Trail continues across the mountain, then descends to Billfish Pond, ending at the Five Ponds Trail. Just above the pond, a side trail leads steeply downhill to where Billfish Brook lazily flows out of the pond and into a narrow gorge. The stream drops abruptly out of the gorge and rushes toward Grand Lake Matagamon. The trail doesn't follow the stream through the gorge. Bushwhacking is difficult and not recommended. It's a pretty place to sit on warm, rough bedrock and contemplate the interplay between rock and water.

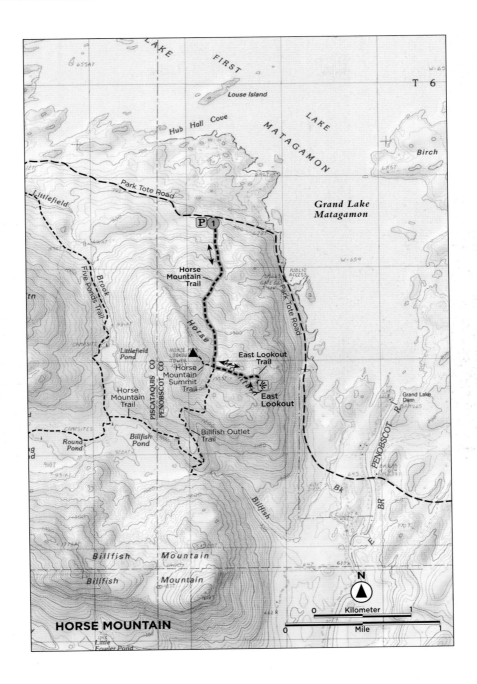

HORSE MOUNTAIN

Looking north from East Lookout

MILES AND DIRECTIONS

0.0   Start from the Horse Mountain Trailhead at the back of the parking area.

1.1   Turn left onto the East Lookout Trail.

1.5   The trail ends at the East Lookout. To complete the hike, return the way you came. **OPTIONS:** At 175 feet south of the junction of the Horse Mountain Trail and the East Lookout Trail, a side trail leads 0.2 mile to Horse Mountain's wooded summit. The Horse Mountain Trail continues south 1.7 miles across and off Horse Mountain to the Five Ponds Trail, passing Billfish Pond. At 0.9 mile from the East Lookout Trail junction, a side trail leads 0.1 mile to Billfish Brook, where it disappears into a narrow gorge.

3.0   Arrive back at the trailhead.

2. TROUT BROOK MOUNTAIN

WHY GO?

Trout Brook Mountain is part of the mass of rhyolite bedrock that includes all the mountains in northeastern Baxter State Park. The hike climbs steadily with several open ledges, offering views north across Grand Lake Matagamon and of the scattered mountains of Aroostook County. The open areas along the trail and the summit are covered with blueberries. As you munch blueberries on the summit, you can look south, through the ever-growing forest, to The Traveler.

THE RUN DOWN

Start: From the Trout Brook Mountain Trailhead.

Elevation gain: 1,154 feet.

Distance: 2.5 miles out and back.

Hiking time: 2-3 hours.

Difficulty: Moderate.

Seasons: June-Sept are best.

Trail surface: Woodland path.

Nearest town: Patten.

Other users: None.

Water availability: None.

Other maps: *DeLorme's The Maine Atlas and Gazetteer* map 51.

Nat Geo TOPO! Map (USGS): Trout Brook Mountain.

Nat Geo Trails Illustrated Map: Baxter State Park.

FINDING THE TRAILHEAD

From the north entrance of Baxter State Park at the Matagamon Gate, drive 2.6 miles on the Tote Road. Just past the entrance to the Trout Brook Farm campground, turn left into the grassy parking area. The trail begins at the sign at the south end of the parking area. The Five Ponds Trailheads are at the east and west ends of the parking area.

Trailhead GPS: N46° 09.817' / W68° 51.138'.

WHAT TO SEE

The trail up Trout Brook Mountain climbs steadily up the mountain's northern flank through a mixed forest to the first set of ledges. The ledge is a steep section of the ridge that won't hold soil, exposing the crumbling rhyolite bedrock. All the mountains from Trout Brook Mountain south to Russell Pond are the remnants of an ancient volcanic eruption. Gnarled scrub pines grow around the ledge, their

Trout Brook Mountain's summit

needles mixing with the crumbled rock on the trail. Even in the wettest times, this section of the trail seems sere.

From the ledges, you have a fine view to the north, across Grand Lake Matagamon. Isolated mountains dot the forested landscape. To the east are Sugarloaf and Mount Chase. To the north the mountains of Aroostook County, including Quaggy Joe and Deboullie. Below you is the open grassy meadow of Trout Brook Farm. Today, it's a campground, but historically this was the center of huge logging operations. The farm was originally cleared around 1837. Farms like Trout Brook Farm and Nesowadnehunk Field were used to supply feed for the animals used in logging and food to supplement the loggers' diet. In its heyday, the farm had numerous hay meadows and barns. In the forest beyond the farm, was a small town that sprang up around a lumber mill. Most of the building was destroyed by a fire in 1903 that burned a swath of forest from Wassataquoik Stream over The Traveler and into the Freezeout area

Grand Lake Matagamon from Trout Brook Mountain Trail

northwest of Trout Brook Farm. After the fire, the farm grew seedling trees to be transplanted to burned over areas. As timbering practices changed, the farms fell into disuse. By the time this northern area became part of Baxter State Park, the farm and the nearby mill had been all but abandoned, and the forest had begun to return.

The trail crosses several open bedrock ledges as you climb. After each ledge—with its view northward—the trail drops back into the woods. It's like a mountain roller coaster: steep, dry rock ledges alternating with a cool, moist forest. The ledges are covered with dry lichen, scrub pine, and blueberries. The woods are full of scattered wildflowers like blue-bead lilies and bunchberry beneath hardwoods and some evergreens.

The summit of the mountain is semi-open with views to the south and west. Beyond the nearly vertical north face of Trout Brook Mountain lies the valley of the five ponds, but to get a view of the ponds you need to descend on the Trout Brook Mountain Trail beyond the summit. From the summit itself, you can see the mountains across the valley: Billfish and Bald Mountains and Barrell Ridge. Beyond them looms The Traveler. All of these mountains are part of the same mass of rhyolite as Trout Brook Mountain. To the west, the Trout Brook valley opens into the endless forest of the Allagash County.

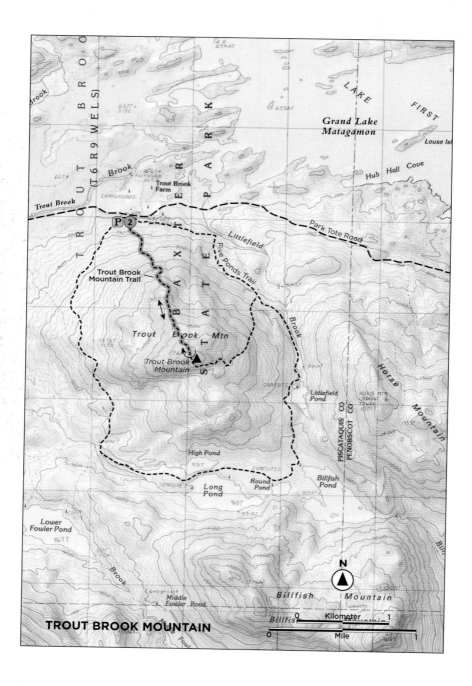

TROUT BROOK MOUNTAIN

Looking south from Trout Brook Mountain's summit

MILES AND DIRECTIONS

0.0 Start from the Trout Brook Mountain Trailhead at the south end of the parking area.

0.7 The trail climbs steadily through the woods to the first set of ledges with views to north.

1.3 The trail climbs several ledges, followed by short descents into the woods until climbing to the semi-open summit with views to the south. To complete the hike as described, return to the trailhead the way you came. **OPTION:** The Trout Brook Mountain Trail continues another 1.0 mile, descending to the Five Ponds Trail. If you turn left onto that trail and follow it back to the trailhead, you'll hike a 3.3-mile loop.

2.5 Arrive back at the trailhead.

3. FIVE PONDS LOOP

WHY GO?

The Five Ponds Trail loops around Trout Brook Mountain through a mostly hardwood forest. You pass each pond and cross a long, rocky esker. Two of the ponds have rental canoes you can use if you get a key from the ranger's station at Trout Brook Farm. The ponds rest in a steep sided valley between rocky mountains.

THE RUN DOWN

Start: From the Five Ponds Trailhead at the east end of the parking area.

Elevation gain: 1,120 feet.

Distance: 7.0 miles loop.

Hiking time: 4–5 hours.

Difficulty: Moderate, because of the distance.

Seasons: June–Sept are best.

Trail surface: Woodland path.

Nearest town: Patten.

Other users: None.

Water availability: Any of the five ponds.

Other maps: DeLorme's The Maine Atlas and Gazetteer map 51.

Nat Geo TOPO! Map (USGS): Trout Brook Mountain.

Nat Geo Trails Illustrated Map: Baxter State Park.

FINDING THE TRAILHEAD

From the north entrance of Baxter State Park at the Matagamon Gate, drive 2.6 miles on the Tote Road. Just past the entrance to the Trout Brook Farm campground, turn left into the grassy parking area. The trail begins at the sign at the east end of the parking area. The Trout Brook Mountain Trailhead and the other end of the Five Ponds Trail are at the west end of the parking area.

Trailhead GPS: N46° 09.820' / W68° 51.118'.

WHAT TO SEE

The Five Ponds Trail circumnavigates Trout Brook Mountain through a mostly hardwood forest. The first pond, Littlefield, is shallow and swampy. Young evergreens, like perfect Christmas trees, gather behind its boggy fringe.

Next, you pass Billfish Pond, nestled in a shallow valley between Billfish and Horse Mountains. It's named for William Fish, an early lumberman, and not reflective of the quality of fishing in the pond. It's the largest of the five ponds. A side trail leads through the campsite to the pond where waves lap at the rocky shore. There's a

Billfish Pond

rental canoe. If you want to explore the pond, the ranger at Trout Brook Farm takes payment and gives you a key to unlock the boat, paddles, and life vests.

From Billfish Pond, the trail climbs an Esker. You walk through the marshy woods, high and dry. The esker, rising about 20 feet above the forest floor, runs roughly east–west for more than 1.0 mile. Through the trees to the north, you get occasional glimpses of Trout Brook Mountain's rocky shoulder. To the south, Round Pond lies between the esker and Billfish Mountain's steeply wooded flank. As you hike along, it's hard to tell where Billfish Pond ended and Round Pond began.

The esker narrows, passing between High and Long Ponds. Two side trails lead to campsites on Long Pond: The second has a rental canoe. In a break in the esker, where an occasional stream connects the two ponds, you reach the jumbled rocks along High Pond's shore. The plaintive cry of loons breaks the natural still.

Past the ponds, the trail descends off the esker and follows a low ridge before turning north. You cross a wide, wooded valley, passing a beaver flowage and an old pond gone to meadow. The trail climbs across the rocky shoulder of Trout Brook Mountain. The last easy mile gives you time to think about how different each of the five ponds are. And how very different they're compared to the string of ponds along the southern end of Baxter.

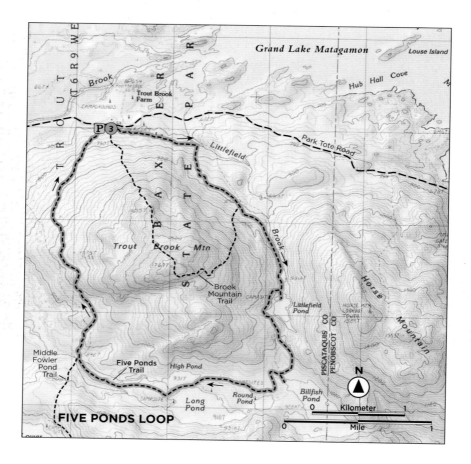

MILES AND DIRECTIONS

0.0   Start from the Five Ponds Trailhead at the east end of the parking area.

1.1   Pass the Trout Brook Mountain Trail.

1.5   The trail follows Littlefield Brook.

2.0   Go straight on the side trail to Littlefield Pond.

2.1   The side trail ends on the shore of the pond. To continue the hike, return to the Five Ponds Trail.

Rocky shoulder of
Trout Brook Mountain
across High Pond

2.2 Turn left back onto the Five Ponds Trail.

2.9 Pass the Horse Mountain Trail.

3.0 Turn left onto the side trail to Billfish Pond.

3.1 The trail passes through a campsite and descends to the pond.
To continue the hike, return to the Five Ponds Trail.

3.2 Turn left back onto the Five Ponds Trail.

4.2 The trail follows the top of an esker to the point where High and Long
Ponds almost touch.

4.3 Turn left onto a short side trail to Long Pond. To continue the hike, return
to the Five Ponds Trail and turn left.

4.4 Pass Middle Fowler Pond Trail.

5.0 Pass Lower Fowler Pond Connector Trail.

7.0 Arrive back at the trailhead.

4. MIDDLE FOWLER POND

WHY GO?

This hike follows a dry ridge to Lower Fowler Pond, a good-sized pond nestled against the slope of Barrell Ridge. You continue on to Middle Fowler Pond. From its shore are fine views of Bald Mountain, North Traveler, and Barrell Ridge. Fowler Brook flows over a beaver dam, out of the pond, and down a series of bedrock pillows.

THE RUN DOWN

Start: From the Fowler Brook Trailhead on the south side of the Park Tote Road.

Elevation gain: 962 feet.

Distance: 6.0 miles out and back.

Hiking time: 3–4 hours.

Difficulty: Easy.

Seasons: May–Oct are best.

Trail surface: Woodland path.

Nearest town: Patten.

Other users: None.

Water availability: Lower and Middle Fowler Ponds.

Other maps: *DeLorme's The Maine Atlas and Gazetteer* map 51.

Nat Geo TOPO! Map (USGS): Frost Pond.

Nat Geo Trails Illustrated Map: Baxter State Park.

FINDING THE TRAILHEAD

From the Matagamon Gate, drive 4.7 miles on the Park Tote Road. There's parking on both sides of the road. The trailhead is on the left.
Trailhead GPS: N46° 08.886' / W68° 52.578'.

WHAT TO SEE

The Fowler Brook Trail follows the brook upstream to Lower Fowler Pond. Mostly the trail stays on dry ledges, winding above the boggy stream. The pond rests in a mixed forest that rises to the southwest up the irregular slope of Barrell Ridge. Unlike most ponds in Baxter, the shore and shallows aren't lined with boulders. The rich green forest comes right down to the water, creating a sharp border between the two.

You hike along the north shore of the pond to a rocky overlook, before turning north. The Fowler Brook Trail ends at the Middle Fowler Pond Trail. As you hike on, you catch glimpses of Lower Fowler Pond through the trees. After climbing a low rise, you begin to hear glimpses of Fowler Brook rushing between the two ponds.

Bald Mountain across
Middle Fowler Pond

Just before Middle Fowler Pond, the trail crosses a bluff overlooking the stream sluicing down pillows of bedrock. Rather than climb down here, hike ahead and access the stream from above. The trail crosses the stream a few feet below Middle Fowler Pond. You step across on large boulders to an open expanse of bedrock. Across the pond, untrailed Bald Mountain juts into the sky.

Take time to explore the stream, the beaver dam at its head, and the campsite on the north shore. From the campsite, you have a fine view of Barrell Ridge across the pond. There's no trail to the third Fowler Pond, a small round lozenge of cold water tucked into the valley between Billfish and Bald Mountains.

The trail continues over the shoulder of Barrell Ridge and on to Lower South Branch Pond in 3.7 miles. The climb to the notch between Barrell Ridge and North Traveler is almost 1,000 feet, climbing from rill to rill in cool woods.

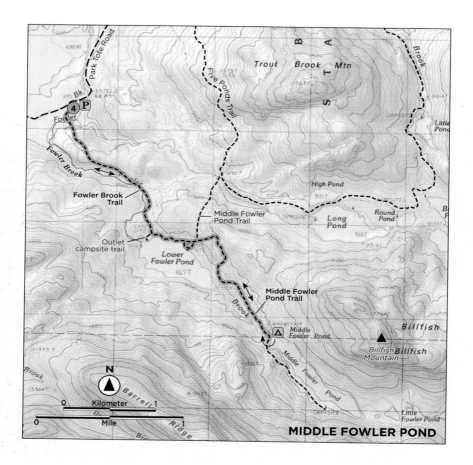

MIDDLE FOWLER POND

MILES AND DIRECTIONS

0.0 Start from the Fowler Brook Trailhead on the south side of the Park Tote Road.

1.4 Arrive at Lower Fowler Pond. A side trail leads west to outlet campsite.

1.7 The trail follows the north shore of the pond. Pass a blazed, but unsigned trail that bypasses the Lower Fowler Pond campsite.

1.8 Pass through the campsite. Beyond the campsite, turn left away from the pond.

1.9 Pass the other end of the bypass trail.

2.1 The Fowler Brook Trail ends at the Middle Fowler Pond Trail. Turn right.

Barrell Ridge across Lower Fowler Pond

3.0   Arrive at Middle Fowler Pond. The trail continues across the outlet
stream another 4.6 miles to South Branch Road near the South Branch
day-use parking area. To complete this hike, return the way you came.
OPTION: Continue on Middle Fowler Trail 3.8 miles to Lower South
Branch Pond, making a 6.8-mile shuttle hike.

6.0   Arrive back at the trailhead.

5. BARRELL RIDGE

WHY GO?

Barrell Ridge's long open summit offers extraordinary views of the surrounding country—lakes, ponds, rocky mountains, and the endless North Woods. The trail passes across open ridges with views and blueberries.

THE RUN DOWN

Start: From the Ledges Trailhead, 300 feet back up South Branch Road from the day-use parking area.

Elevation gain: 1,563 feet.

Distance: 6.0 miles out and back.

Hiking time: 3–4 hours.

Difficulty: Moderate.

Seasons: May–Oct are best.

Trail surface: Woodland path.

Nearest town: Patten.

Other users: None.

Water availability: None.

Other maps: *DeLorme's The Maine Atlas and Gazetteer* map 51.

Nat Geo TOPO! Map (USGS): Wassataquoik Lake.

Nat Geo Trails Illustrated Map: Baxter State Park.

FINDING THE TRAILHEAD

From the Matagamon Gate, drive 7.0 miles on the Park Tote Road. Turn left onto South Branch Road. Drive 2.2 miles to the day-use parking area. The trailhead is 300 feet back up the road.

Trailhead GPS: N46° 06.563' / W68° 54.101'.

WHAT TO SEE?

Barrell Ridge runs northwest to southeast, separated from North Traveler by Dry Brook's steep valley. The mostly open summit offers, in the words of one of the trail signs, extraordinary views.

The Middle Fowler Pond Trail climbs steadily from South Branch Valley through mature hardwoods. After a short, steep climb, you reach the shoulder of Little Peaked Mountain. Hardwoods give way to evergreens. The trail slabs around, then follows a relatively flat ridge top. In several places, the ridge is open with views of Barrell Ridge and the North Woods. Blueberries and bunchberries crowd the openings.

Barrell Ridge from Middle
Fowler Pond Trail

As you climb toward the notch between Barrell Ridge and North Traveler, the trail crosses Dry Brook. To your right, off the trail is a cascade. In the notch, you reach the Barrell Ridge Trail.

The climb to the summit is short and very steep in places. The trail crosses from one open bedrock slab to the next. As you climb, the views become more expansive. The high point on the ridge is at the southeast end where the trail ends. Take time to explore the semi-open summit ridge, taking care to stay on the rocks and not trample the fragile vegetation.

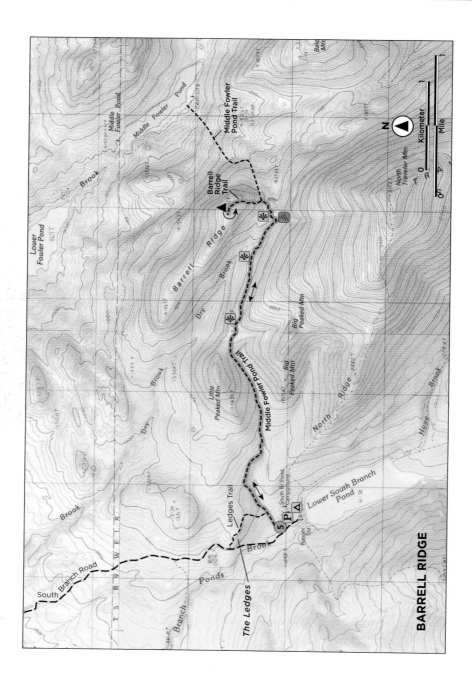

BARRELL RIDGE

Morning fog obscuring Bald Mountain
seen from Barrell Ridge

MILES AND DIRECTIONS

0.0 Start from the Ledges Trailhead, 300 feet back up South Branch Road from the day-use parking area.

0.2 Continue straight onto the Middle Fowler Pond Trail.

1.6 The trail climbs steadily to the notch between Little Peaked Mountain and Big Peaked Mountain with fine views west and north.

2.1 The trail slabs along the shoulder of the North Traveler to an open overlook.

2.5 The trail crosses, then follows Dry Brook. Where the trail turns uphill away from the stream, there's a small, picturesque waterfall just off the trail.

2.6 The trail climbs to the notch between Barrell Ridge and North Traveler with fine views across the valley of Barrell Ridge.

2.7 Turn left onto the Barrell Ridge Trail.

3.0 Climb with increasingly fine views to the summit of Barrell Ridge. To complete the hike, return the way you came.

6.0 Arrive back at the trailhead.

6. SOUTH BRANCH FALLS

WHY GO?
An easy hike leads to the falls, less a waterfall than a quarter-mile race. The water churns through and around rifts in the slate bedrock. The trail crosses the rock with fine views. There are several holes and a large pool good for swimming.

THE RUN DOWN

Start: From the South Branch Falls Trailhead at the back of the parking area.

Elevation gain: 216 feet on the return hike.

Distance: 1.0 mile out and back.

Hiking time: About 1 hour.

Difficulty: Easy.

Seasons: May–Oct are best.

Trail surface: Woodland path.

Nearest town: Patten.

Other users: None.

Water availability: None.

Other maps: *DeLorme's The Maine Atlas and Gazetteer* map 51.

Nat Geo TOPO! Map (USGS): Wassataquoik Lake.

Nat Geo Trails Illustrated Map: Baxter State Park.

FINDING THE TRAILHEAD

 From the Matagamon Gate, drive 7.0 miles on the Park Tote Road. Turn left onto South Branch Road. Drive 1.3 miles. The trailhead parking is on the left. The trailhead is at the back of the parking area.
Trailhead GPS: N46° 07.211' / W68° 54.367'.

WHAT TO SEE
South Branch Falls is less a waterfall than a quarter-mile race. The stream churns along the edge of a huge hump of bedrock. It slides through narrow V-shaped joints in the slate, drops into deep swirling pools, and crosses ledges, erratically following the route of least resistance.

The hike to the falls is short and flat. Just before the falls, there's a steep descent to the bedrock hump. The trail crosses the bedrock from where the water pools up before racing through the falls to where it relaxes into a wide, calm pool with strings of bubbles eddying into the distance.

The pool below the falls and the larger pools within the falls offer hot hikers a cool summer respite. After a bracing swim, you can dry and warm on the rough, bare

The water follows seams
in the tilted bedrock

rock. It's understandable that you might be tempted to jump into the water from one of the cliffs. Don't be! Most of the race is too narrow and swift for safe swimming.

While you are relaxing on the rocks, be sure to take in the surrounding forest. In spring, the hardwoods are various fresh greens, tinted with red or yellow. In fall, the woods explode with color. Varied wildflowers bloom across the seasons, attracting pollinators and songbirds. And always, the water rushes noisily through the falls.

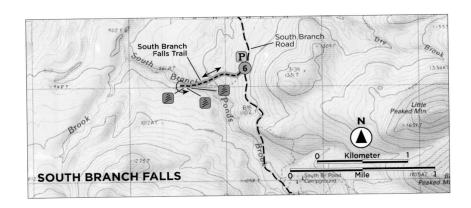

SOUTH BRANCH FALLS

South Branch Falls empties into a large pool

MILES AND DIRECTIONS

0.0 Start from the trailhead at the back of the parking area.

0.4 The trail descends to a large dome of rock. Follow the blazes over the rock, stopping to explore the stream below.

0.5 The trail descends off the bedrock dome and ends on a finger of rock that juts out into South Branch Ponds Brook below the falls. To complete the hike, return the way you came.

1.0 Arrive back at the trailhead.

7. HOWE BROOK FALLS

WHY GO?

The Howe Brook Trail follows Howe Brook from near where it flows into Lower South Branch Pond upstream past lower falls and on to upper falls. The lower falls is a long series of drops, pool, and sluices over and around exposed bedrock. It offers several large swimming holes and sunny flat rocks to dry out on. The upper falls is a single drop off a cliff that arcs across the valley. Just below the upper falls, you can explore Howe Brook off trail. The section of the brook just below the upper falls is much like the lower falls, except even more vertical.

THE RUN DOWN

Start: From the day-use parking area at the end of the South Branch Pond Road.

Elevation gain: 964 feet.

Distance: 6.1 miles out and back.

Hiking time: 3–4 hours.

Difficulty: Moderate.

Seasons: June–Oct are best.

Trail surface: Woodland path.

Nearest town: Patten.

Other users: None.

Water availability: Lower South Branch Pond near the trailhead and Howe Brook.

Other maps: *DeLorme's The Maine Atlas and Gazetteer* map 51.

Nat Geo TOPO! Map (USGS): Wassataquoik Lake.

Nat Geo Trails Illustrated Map: Baxter State Park.

FINDING THE TRAILHEAD

From the north entrance of Baxter State Park at the Matagamon Gate, drive 7.0 miles on the Tote Road. Turn left onto the South Branch Pond Road at the sign for South Branch Pond. Drive 1.9 miles to the end of the road where the day-use parking is. Begin the hike by walking into the campground past the ranger's station.
Trailhead GPS: N46° 06.518' / W68° 54.050'.

WHAT TO SEE

The landscape of Baxter State Park is one shaped by water. Most famously, the glaciers of the last ice age scraped the mountains down to bedrock and left the nearly vertical-sided bowls of the basins of Katahdin. But, in fact, as the earth warmed and

Upper Howe Brook Falls

the ice retreated, water continued shaping the land. You can see this being played out along the hike to Howe Brook Falls.

The first you see of Howe Brook, near where it flows into Lower South Branch Pond, has a wide bed of football-sized rocks. All worn round over time as the flowing water jostled them against one another. Most of the summer, the stream almost disappears beneath the rocks, making for easy, dry crossing. In the spring, overflowing with snowmelt, Howe Brook rages between its banks. Even after a hard summer rain, the water rises over the rocks, making a crossing a cold, wet prospect. The sound of the stream rushing over the rocks fills the whole valley between The Traveler and South Branch Mountain.

The lower falls isn't one waterfall but several hundred yards of drops, pools, and sluices. The water backs up behind an exposed mass of bedrock and either slides in thin sheets over the rock or finds a weakness in the rock and creates a crack that the water widens year by year. The pools collect rounded rocks visible through the

A hiker contemplates swimming in Lower Howe Brook Falls

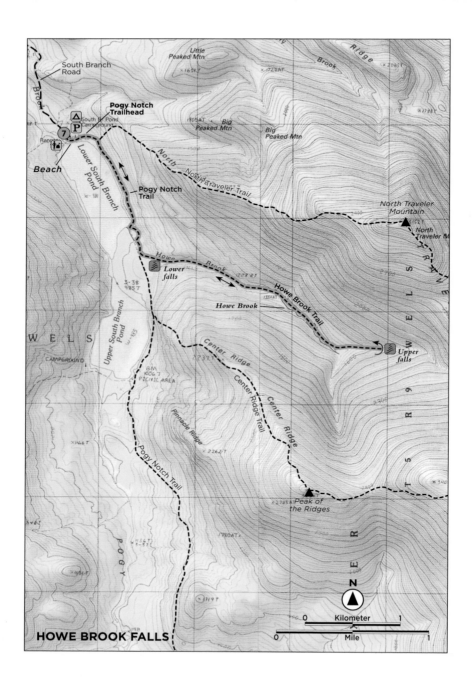

South Branch Road

Little Peaked Mtn

Ridge

Brook

Pogy Notch Trailhead

South B. Pond Campground

7 P

Beach

Lower South Branch Pond

Pogy Notch Trail

Big Peaked Mtn

Big Peaked Mtn

North

North Traveler Trail

North Traveler Mountain

North Traveler M

Howe Brook

Lower falls

Howe Brook Trail

Howe Brook

Upper falls

Upper South Branch Pond

CAMPGROUND

BM PICNIC AREA

W E L S

Center Ridge

Center Ridge Trail

Center Ridge

Pinnacle Ridge

Pogy Notch Trail

Peak of the Ridges

P · O · G · Y

R 9 5 T

E R

N

Kilometer
0   1

Mile
0   1

HOWE BROOK FALLS

crystal clear water. In places, the stream has undercut overhanging rock faces, creating shaded pools overhung by cedars. Mostly, the lower falls is a sunny place with expanses of bare bedrock. The rock is kept smooth and clear by annual scourings of spring runoff. During the summer, they make for a great place to sit and sun after a dip in one of the coolest pools.

The trail beyond the lower falls is washed out in several places, forcing you to either step from stone to stone in the streambed or struggle on the steep slopes above Howe Brook on the rerouted trail. These washouts occur on the outside of bends in the stream, where the water beats on the stream bank, trying to go straight rather than bend with streambed. Over time, the stream gets wider and rockier. The hardwood trees of the surrounding forest hold the bank in place with their roots. Roots and rocks stick out of the undercut banks, as the smaller, lighter soil and rocks fall away.

The upper falls is a single drop off a 20-foot cliff that arcs from bank to bank. You can see the bedding in the rock and its uneven weathering—very different from the smooth, hard rock at the lower falls. Just downstream from the upper falls, the bedrock is more like that around lower falls. If you explore downstream, you'll see where the stream flows through a series of cracks in the bedrock. Some are still very narrow, while others have widened to where you would not call them cracks any longer.

High above Howe Brook, unseen through the hardwood forest, rise the several peaks of The Traveler. The mountain makes a half circle around Howe Brook's valley. The bare summits of the mountain are rhyolite in various stages of weathering. The hard, volcanic rhyolite originated in the same volcanic activity as the smooth bedrock of the lower falls. Glaciers scoured out the valley Howe Brook flows down to Lower South Branch Pond, and now the stream continues to eat into the bedrock, year by year altering the course of the stream and carrying more and more of the mountain down to the pond. In our lifetimes, these changes are small and seen only in the rearranging of rock in the streambed and the undercutting of the stream's banks.

MILES AND DIRECTIONS

0.0 Start by walking past the ranger's station and through the campground.

0.2 Turn right onto the Pogy Notch Trail. Remember to sign in at the trailhead.

0.3 Pass the North Traveler Mountain Trail.

0.9 The trail circles around Lower South Branch Pond to a small beach where canoeists leave their boats to continue on foot.

1.0 Turn left onto Howe Brook Trail.

1.2 The trail follows the stream to the beginning of the lower falls. Lower falls is a series of drops, pools, and sluices that continue for more than 0.1 mile.

3.1 The trail follows Howe Brook, turning away from the stream to make the last climb to the upper falls where the trail ends. Be sure to explore Howe Brook downstream from the falls where it drops through a series of sluices. To complete the hike, return the way you came to the trailhead.

6.1 Arrive back at the trailhead.

8. THE TRAVELER

WHY GO?

The Traveler is as long and difficult a hike as Katahdin. Because of the difference in geology, the two mountains feel very different. The hiking is very different, too. The Traveler is never crowded; most days you have the mountain almost to yourself. Even though all of The Traveler is part of a huge mass of rhyolite, the four peaks the hike crosses all feel and look unique. Much of the hike is spent on open slopes and summits with views in every direction and blueberries everywhere.

THE RUN DOWN

Start: From the day-use parking area at the end of the South Branch Ponds Road.

Elevation gain: 4,094 feet.

Distance: 10.1 miles loop.

Hiking time: 7–9 hours.

Difficulty: Most strenuous.

Seasons: June–Sept are best.

Trail surface: Woodland path with long sections above tree line.

Nearest town: Patten.

Other users: None.

Water availability: Lower South Branch Pond near the trailhead and Howe Brook at mile 1.0.

Other maps: *DeLorme's The Maine Atlas and Gazetteer* map 51.

Nat Geo TOPO! Map (USGS): Wassataquoik Lake.

Nat Geo Trails Illustrated Map: Baxter State Park.

FINDING THE TRAILHEAD

From the north entrance of Baxter State Park at the Matagamon Gate, drive 7.0 miles on the Tote Road. Turn left onto the South Branch Pond Road at the sign for South Branch Pond. Drive 1.9 miles to the end of the road where the day-use parking is. Begin the hike by walking into the campground past the ranger's station.
Trailhead GPS: N46° 06.518' / W68° 54.050'.

WHAT TO SEE

Around 400 million years ago, the ancient supercontinent Avalonia collided with North America. During this geologically active period, the granites of Maine were laid down. It was also when an ancient volcano erupted and huge ash flows—a mineral called tuff—covered the area north of what is today Katahdin. The heat and

The Traveler's main summit
from Little Knife Edge

pressure of successive layers of ash flow compacted and metamorphosed the older layers. The rock that was created is called rhyolite. It's related to granite, but is harder and finer grained. Like granite, as the rhyolite cooled, it developed shrinkage fractures. Many of the formations you see on The Traveler resulted from the aging and weathering along these fracture lines. Unlike granite, rhyolite tends to break apart and crumble along the fracture lines. As a result, much of The Traveler seems to be little more than a giant pile of loose rocks. The Traveler is at the heart of this huge mass of rhyolite that also includes Black Cat and South Branch Mountains to the west and all the mountains north of Traveler in Baxter State Park. The mass of rhyolite is more than 10,000 feet thick and is made of at least 80 cubic miles of bedrock.

The Traveler has four peaks: Peak of the Ridges, Traveler Peak, Traveler Ridge, and North Traveler. The hike crosses all four. Each is unique in appearance even though they're all part of the same rhyolite formation. This is in large part because of geological forces that deformed the rock since it was formed and weathering that has occurred more recently.

The Center Ridge Trail climbs steeply up toward Peak of the Ridges. As you climb, the views open up and the trail becomes almost entirely loose rocks. The peaks that stick up out of the ridge are rhyolite masses with abundant shrinkage fractures. The fractures tended to create hexagonal columns of rock packed together. The varying size of the hexagons is a function of how quickly the rock cooled. Among the rocks, in protected pockets where soil has accumulated, blueberries and mountain ash flourish.

The hexagons are very obvious on the summit of Peak of the Ridges—that is if you can tear yourself away from the view to look at them. Beyond Turner and Wassataquoik Mountains, Katahdin looms. The North Peaks blocks a clear view of the Great Basin, but the Knife Edge stands out against the horizon. Farther west, is

Peak of Ridges from the main summit

the jumble of mountains that include Doubletop, The Brothers, and Mullen Mountain. To the east, the scree-covered slopes of Traveler Peak rise to its long and irregular summit ridge. To the north, across Howe Brook Valley, the long ridge of North Traveler blocks everything beyond it.

From The Peak of the Ridges, the trail descends a rocky ridge that drops steeply on both sides—especially the south. The ridge is called Little Knife Edge for its resemblance to the larger, more famous formation on Katahdin. The shrinkage fractures are very noticeable where the trail crosses atop the ridge.

The trail drops down into a wooded saddle, passing through a forest of smallish fir—a cool, shady respite from the open ridges of the last several miles. The ascent up Traveler Peak is on mostly loose, football-sized and larger rocks. The summit offers the same views as Peak of the Ridges with the addition of the East Branch Penobscot River winding through the woods below you to the east. It's the view of The Traveler from the East Branch that gave the mountain its name. Because The Traveler is such a large, irregularly shaped mountain and because the East Branch takes such a sinuous course beneath it, early river drivers felt the mountain was moving, traveling along with them. Beyond the river are Sugarloaf and Mount Chase: two isolated mountains that aren't part of the Traveler Rhyolite.

The descent off Traveler Peak is steep, but mostly not on loose rocks. There are abundant blueberries as well as numerous alpine plants, including mountain cranberry. After dropping into the woods to a noticeable notch, the trail climbs gently to cross Traveler Ridge. The ridge is mostly open with views north around North Traveler to the mountains of the Five Ponds area. After crossing the unmarked high point on the ridge, the trail drops steeply down into a forest of birch to, again, a noticeable notch.

The climb up to the summit of North Traveler is surprisingly short and easy. The summit seems to be nothing more than a large pile of loose rocks. The rhyolite here has broken into smaller, flatter pieces that have weathered to a dusty orange due to iron in the rock.

The long descent to Lower South Branch Pond alternates between a birch forest, a grassy meadow, an exposed bedrock clifftop, and loose rock slides. Take your time and enjoy the varied and many views. Far below you, canoes and kayaks move around the pond. You may even see a moose swimming across the pond. Just before the trail drops into the woods for good, you get one last view of Katahdin on the horizon through Pogy Notch.

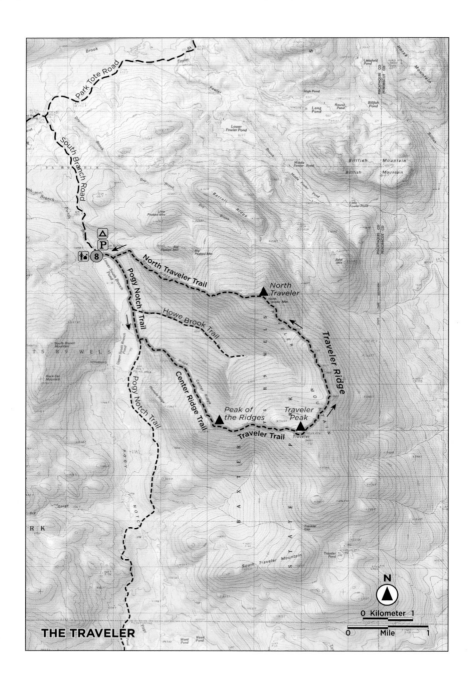

THE TRAVELER

MILES AND DIRECTIONS

0.0 Start by walking past the ranger's station and through the campground.

0.2 Turn right off the campground road onto the Pogy Notch Trail.

0.3 Pass the North Traveler Trail.

1.0 The Pogy Notch Trail follows the shore of Lower South Branch Pond in the woods a hundred yards back from the pond. Just past the south end of the pond, pass the Howe Brook Trail and cross Howe Brook. In the spring and after a rain, you'll have to wade across the stream.

2.1 The trail crosses the woods between Lower and Upper South Branch Ponds. Just when Upper South Branch Pond becomes visible through the trees, the trail bears left and climbs a rock face to the junction with Center Ridge Trail. The junction is in a grove of red pines atop a high cliff that drops straight down into Upper South Branch Pond. Turn left onto Center Ridge Trail.

2.8 The trail climbs very steeply, then switchbacks up the rocky ridge to the first peak on the ridge with views in every direction.

3.4 The trail climbs steadily over two other peaks to Peak of the Ridges. The trail is often over loose rocks and boulders among blueberries and mountain ash. The Center Ridge Trail ends on Peak of the Ridges. The trail continues as the Traveler Trail.

4.0 The trail descends steeply down a rock spine into the wooded saddle between Peak of the Ridges and Traveler Peak.

4.7 The trail climbs steadily up loose rocks and small groves of stunted trees to Traveler Peak.

5.4 The trail descends steeply to a wooded notch between Traveler Peak and Traveler Ridge.

6.3 The trail climbs gently to the long open summit of Traveler Ridge. The unmarked high point of Traveler Ridge is at its far north end.

6.7 The trail descends steeply through birch to the notch between Traveler Ridge and North Traveler.

7.4 The trail climbs steadily along rock spines to North Traveler's summit, which is little more than a pile of small, broken rocks. The Traveler Trail ends on the summit. The trail continues as North Traveler Trail.

9.8 The North Traveler Trail descends steadily, passing in and out of wooded areas and across open cliff tops. On the steepest sections, the trail is covered with small, loose rocks. After a particularly steep section with a fine view south through Pogy Notch of Katahdin, the trail drops into the woods and descends steadily to Pogy Notch Trail. Turn right to head back to the trailhead.

10.1 Arrive back at the day-use parking area.

9. BLACK CAT MOUNTAIN

WHY GO?

Black Cat Mountain's open summit offers one of the most expansive views in Baxter State Park. The climb is very steep in places, but worth the effort. Along the way, there's an overlook on the shoulder of South Branch Mountain, but no view from its summit.

THE RUN DOWN

Start: From the South Branch Mountain Trailhead at the west end of the beach behind the ranger's station.

Elevation gain: 2,133 feet.

Distance: 6.0 miles out and back.

Difficulty: More strenuous.

Seasons: June–Oct are best.

Trail surface: Woodland path.

Nearest town: Patten.

Other users: None.

Water availability: Lower South Branch Pond at the trailhead.

Other maps: *DeLorme's The Maine Atlas and Gazetteer* map 51.

Nat Geo TOPO! Map (USGS): Wassataquoik Lake.

Nat Geo Trails Illustrated Map: Baxter State Park.

FINDING THE TRAILHEAD

From the Matagamon Gate, drive 7.0 miles on the Park Tote Road. Turn left onto South Branch Road. Drive 2.2 miles to the day-use parking area. From the parking area, walk 0.1 mile into the campground to the ranger's station. The trailhead is behind the ranger's station in the day-use area along the lake where South Branch Ponds Brook flows out of Lower South Branch Pond. **Trailhead GPS:** N46° 06.516' / W68° 54.052'.

WHAT TO SEE

From the summit of Black Cat Mountain, you can see pretty much all of Baxter State Park. Across the South Branch Ponds, The Traveler's many peaks circle around Howe Brook. The Traveler reaches south, almost touching the Turners. The jagged indigo outline of Katahdin dominates the southern horizon. Nearer, the Pogy Mountains, the most remote spot east of the Mississippi, sit blanketed in dark forest.

The South Branch Mountain Trail begins where Lower South Branch Pond narrows to a wide, shallow stream and enters an irregular marshy area. Most of the summer, you can cross the stream on stepping stones without getting wet.

Across the stream, the trail follows a small brook, then turns south and begins climbing. The trail becomes steep and rocky. As you climb, partial views begin to

The Traveler from the first overlook

appear—here a glimpse of The Traveler, next South Branch Pond sparkles below you. About a half mile before South Branch Mountain's summit, there's an open ledge with fine views. A great place to stop for a snack and watch vultures and hawks soar on thermals.

South Branch Mountain's summit is a nondescript spot in thick spruce marked with a sign. From there, the trail drops steeply into the notch between South Branch and Black Cat Mountains. Black Cat Mountain is about 100 feet higher than South Branch Mountain, so you'll probably grumble about the descent, knowing you have to make it all up. But somehow, the climb to Black Cat's summit seems shorter and easier. A quick climb out of a birch stand and up a rocky slope and there you are. Mountain ash, berry brambles, and slabs of broken rhyolite dominate the summit.

You can return the way you came or continue on the trail to Upper South Branch Pond. The descent is very steep with lots of loose rocks and soil. Upper South Branch Pond and the marshy area north of it are great places to see moose and ducks.

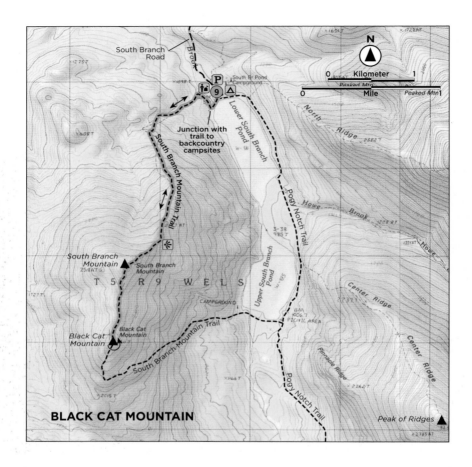

BLACK CAT MOUNTAIN

MILES AND DIRECTIONS

0.0 Follow the gravel road into the campground. Continue down toward Lower South Branch Pond past the ranger's station.

0.1 The trailhead is on the shore of the pond where South Branch Ponds Brook flows out of the lake.

0.2 Ford the stream and pass the side trail to the backcountry campsites.

1.9 The trail is mostly level for the first half mile, then begins climbing steeply. High on the shoulder of South Branch Mountain is a rocky outcropping with fine views.

2.3 Cross the wooded summit of South Branch Mountain.

2.9 Descend off South Branch Mountain and cross to Black Cat Mountain. After a short climb, you emerge on the open summit.

Hikers contemplate The Traveler
from Black Cat Mountain

3.0 You can continue across the summit for better views south. To complete the hike, return the way you came. **OPTION:** You can continue on South Branch Mountain Trail descending to Upper South Branch Pond. The trail ends at Pogy Notch Trail, which you can follow back to the trailhead. This would be a 7.1-mile loop.

6.0 Arrive back at the trailhead.

10. BURNT MOUNTAIN

WHY GO?

The northwestern part of Baxter State Park is characterized by isolated, low mountains. Burnt Mountain is the only trailed one. After a steady but not difficult climb, you have a spectacular view to the south and east from a rocky clearing near the summit.

THE RUN DOWN

Start: From the Burnt Mountain Trailhead at the north end of the parking area.

Elevation gain: 761 feet.

Distance: 2.6 miles out and back.

Hiking time: About 2 hours.

Difficulty: Moderate.

Seasons: May–Oct are best.

Trail surface: Woodland path.

Nearest town: Patten.

Other users: None.

Water availability: None.

Other maps: *DeLorme's The Maine Atlas and Gazetteer* map 50.

Nat Geo TOPO! Map (USGS): Nesowadnehunk Lake.

Nat Geo Trails Illustrated Map: Baxter State Park.

FINDING THE TRAILHEAD

 From the Matagamon Gate, drive 13.4 miles on the Park Tote Road. The Burnt Mountain Trailhead parking is on the left in a small clearing. The trailhead is at the north end of the parking area next to the privy.
Trailhead GPS: N46° 05.934' / W69° 01.247'.

WHAT TO SEE

The forests of Baxter that we see today were shaped by logging and fire. There's little of the original forest left. Several fires swept up the Wassataquoik watershed, burning much of the region in the early Twentieth Century. Presumably, Burnt Mountain got its name from one of those fires. As you hike up the mountain, there's evidence of human use, but not fire. The lower trail seems to be an old woods road, and on the summit are the concrete footers of a long-gone fire tower.

The view of Baxter's most remote mountains from the end of Burnt Mountain Trail

Just beyond the summit, the trail ends at a rocky overlook. The view across McCarty Field is startlingly beautiful. Irregular mountains are everywhere, filling the scene. McCarty, Howe, Strickland, Center, Lord, Sable, and Pogy Mountains are all visible. All are remote and untrailed. It's understandable if you walk out onto the crumbling rock and feel like the first and only soul to see this view—like a beaver-hatted timber cruiser of an earlier century.

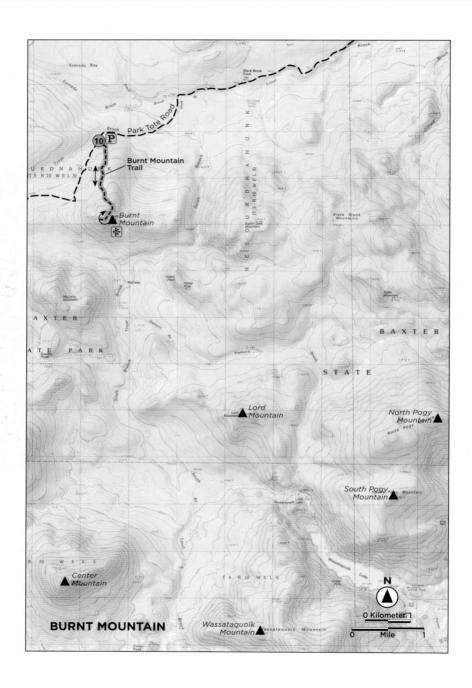

Park Tote Road

10 P

Burnt Mountain
Trail

Burnt
Mountain

Lord
Mountain

North Pogy
Mountain

South Pogy
Mountain

Center
Mountain

N

0 Kilometer 1

0   Mile   1

BURNT MOUNTAIN

Wassataquoik
Mountain

Center Mountain about to be enveloped by an afternoon thunderstorm that already hides the Wassataquoik Mountain

MILES AND DIRECTIONS

0.0 Start from the Burnt Mountain Trailhead at the north end of the parking area.

1.2 The trail climbs gently, then steadily to the semi-open summit.

1.3 Cross the summit to an open overlook with fine views. To complete the hike, return the way you came.

2.6 Arrive back at the trailhead.

11. DWELLEY POND

WHY GO?
Dwelley Pond is a marsh-fringed pond among rounded, forest-covered mountains. It's a good place to see moose and enjoy some North Woods solitude. The hike follows the old McCarty Road, passing the remaining open fields at the site of the old logging camp. The entire hike offers good wildlife-viewing opportunities.

THE RUN DOWN

Start: From the Dwelley Pond North Trailhead.

Elevation gain: 659 feet.

Distance: 7.8 miles out and back or 5.7 miles shuttle hike.

Hiking time: 3–5 hours.

Difficulty: Moderate, due to distance.

Seasons: May–Oct are best.

Trail surface: Old road bed become woodland path.

Nearest town: Jackman.

Other users: None.

Water availability: Dwelley Pond.

Other maps: *DeLorme's The Maine Atlas and Gazetteer* map 50.

Nat Geo TOPO! Map (USGS): Nesowadnehunk Lake.

Nat Geo Trails Illustrated Map: Baxter State Park.

FINDING THE TRAILHEAD

From the Matagamon Gate, drive 14.3 miles on the Park Tote Road. The Dwelley Pond North Trailhead is on the left where the Tote Road bends right. The trailhead is at the south end of the parking area.
Trailhead GPS: N46° 05.227' / W69° 01.611'.

WHAT TO SEE
Northwest Baxter State Park is an area of remote valleys and low, wooded mountains. Along the South Branch of Trout Brook, in the Nineteenth Century, was a logging depot and a farm called McCarty. The Dwelley Pond Trail follows an old roadbed to the McCarty site. Two sets of benches are along the trail for hikers to sit and watch the open fields. Butterflies and birds go about their business. Deer and moose pass through, mostly at twilight. Trout Brook babbles a winding course on the far side of the remaining fields. Across the meadows, rises Howe Peak. Farther south, you can see Lord Mountain; to the north, Burnt Mountain.

McCarty Field

    The trail passes beyond the old logging depot, staying with the roadbed. After turning west, the trail passes numerous abandoned beaver flowages. Old dams moulder, overgrown with touch-me-nots. The ponds have gone boggy or even become grassy swales with gray snags standing in them. Look for wild strawberries growing along the old roadbed. The small, irregular fruits are scarlet drops of summer.

    At Dwelley Pond, there's a privy and a picnic shelter. A side trail leads to a rental canoe and views of the pond. Dwelley Pond is roughly round, fringed by marsh. Watch for ducks, trout, moose, and beaver in the pond. Across the water, rises Morse Mountain. Ironically, the hike loops around three sides of McCarty Mountain, but you never get a view of it.

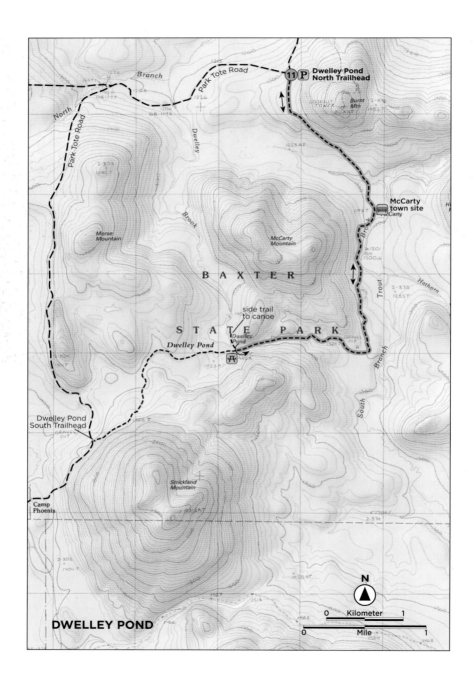

Park Tote Road

Branch

11 P Dwelley Pond
North Trailhead

Burnt
Mtn

North

Park Tote Road

Dwelley

Brook

Morse
Mountain

McCarty
Mountain

McCarty
town site

B A X T E R

S T A T E   P A R K

side trail
to canoe

Dwelley
Pond

Dwelley Pond

Trout

Hathorn

Dwelley Pond
South Trailhead

South Branch

Strickland
Mountain

Camp
Phoenix

N

DWELLEY POND

0   Kilometer   1

0   Mile   1

A small cove on Dwelley Pond from the picnic area

MILES AND DIRECTIONS

0.0 Start from the Dwelley Pond North Trailhead at the south end of the parking area.

1.5 The trail follows an old roadbed to the McCarty town site, where there are two sets of benches and several open fields.

2.0 The trail turns away from South Branch Trout Brook.

3.0 The trail passes an area of numerous old, abandoned beaver flowages.

3.7 Arrive at Dwelley Pond. Turn right onto the Canoe Access Trail.

3.9 Pass the canoe and reach the end of the trail on the pond's shore. Return to Dwelley Pond Trail.

4.1 Arrive back at Dwelley Pond Trail. The picnic area is 250 feet west. A short side trail to the pond is 400 feet west. To complete the hike, turn left and return the way you came. **OPTION:** You can turn right and hike 1.6 miles to the Dwelley Pond South Trailhead on the Park Tote Road, making your hike a 5.7-mile shuttle hike.

7.8 Arrive back at the trailhead.

12. DOUBLETOP MOUNTAIN

WHY GO?

Doubletop Mountain rises west of Nesowadnehunk Stream, across the valley from Mount O-J-I. The two peaks offer fine views of those mountains as well as Katahdin. Situated on the western boundary of Baxter State Park, you can see most of the park from the summit. If you turn away from Katahdin, you can see across the lakes country south and west of the park—an endless sea of deep green punctuated with silver lakes. The middle section of the climb is very steep, but involves only a little rock scrambling.

THE RUN DOWN

Start: From the Doubletop Mountain Trailhead west of the parking area at the sign-in box next to the bridge over Nesowadnehunk Stream.

Elevation gain: 2,393 feet.

Distance: 7.6 miles out and back.

Hiking time: 5–6 hours.

Difficulty: More strenuous.

Seasons: June–Sept are best.

Trail surface: Woodland path.

Nearest town: Millinocket.

Other users: None.

Water availability: Nesowadnehunk Stream at the trailhead and Doubletop Stream at mile 1.8.

Other maps: *DeLorme's The Maine Atlas and Gazetteer* map 50.

Nat Geo TOPO! Map (USGS): Doubletop Mountain.

Nat Geo Trails Illustrated Map: Baxter State Park.

FINDING THE TRAILHEAD

From the south entrance of Baxter State Park at the Togue Pond Gate, drive 16.7 miles on the Tote Road. Turn left into Nesowadnehunk Field campground. The day-use parking is 0.2 mile next to the ranger station, before the end of the road. The trailhead is at the sign-in box next to the bridge over Nesowadnehunk Stream.

Trailhead GPS: N45° 58.570' / W69° 04.696'.

Doubletop Mountain seen from Tote Road at the Slide Dam

WHAT TO SEE

Doubletop Mountain is a narrow ridge that rises sharply above Nesowadnehunk Stream west of Katahdin. Its relative isolation makes it to stand out even more, visible from the Tote Road off and on from Daicey Pond north all the way to Nesowadnehunk Lake. The mountain's east face, the one you see from the road, is so steep that huge areas of it are bare rock. The Doubletop Mountain Trail goes over the mountain from Nesowadnehunk Field to Kidney Pond. But because the south face of the mountain is much steeper than the north ridge, it's easier to climb the mountain from Nesowadnehunk Field and return the same way. You could hike the mountain as a shuttle, but should be warned that the descent off South Peak toward Kidney Pond is among the steepest trails in the state with several rock chimneys that need to be negotiated.

Starting from Nesowadnehunk Field, the trail crosses Nesowadnehunk Stream and passes through the campground. The trail leaves the south end of the campground and follows along the stream. The first mile is an easy climb through hardwoods. After a short, steep descent, the trail crosses Doubletop Stream. This is where the climb begins. At first, the trail climbs through hardwoods, the trail dirt and rocks. Soon the forest transitions to evergreens and the trail becomes rockier with some slabs of bedrock to scale. You begin to get partial views north through the trees.

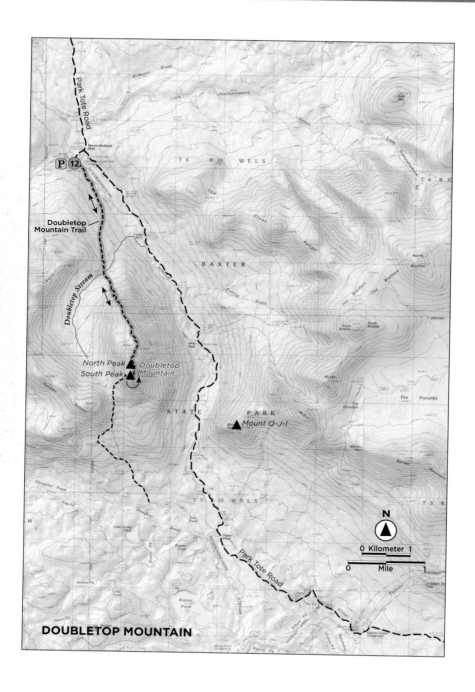

DOUBLETOP MOUNTAIN

Doubletop Mountain seen from Mount O-J-I

After gaining more than 1,200 feet in 0.7 mile, the trail levels out. Just in case you thought you might be on the summit ridge, there's an old sign nailed to a tree, letting you know that the summit is still a mile away. The trail weaves through evergreens and moss, not climbing for much of that mile. After a steep climb that is as much rock scrambling as hiking, you reach the north summit. It's the higher of the two summits. It's a large square boulder that sits on the ridge top, rising above the stunted spruce. The sign marking the summit is 20 feet below you in a small clear area where the trail continues. From the summit, you have fine views of the mountains across Nesowadnehunk Valley: Mount O-J-I, the North and South Brothers, and Mount Coe. Behind them looms the granite mass of Katahdin.

The trail drops down from the peak to the north and loops around, dropping slightly to the narrow saddle between the two peaks. Especially to the east, the ridge drops off nearly vertically. The trail crosses the uneven granite atop the cliffs.

South Peak rises slightly, a large boulder sitting on a sheet of bedrock surrounded by cliffs on three sides. Below, you see a string of ponds that Nesowadnehunk Stream winds between.

The Doubletop Mountain Trail tumbles down the west face of the mountain, trending south toward Kidney Pond. The steepest sections are invisible in the trees that don't quite reach the summit ridge. From below, near Kidney Pond, Doubletop Mountain looks like a nearly perfect triangle, capped with bare granite. This view is looking end-on at the mountain to South Peak. From Ledge Falls, along the Tote Road, between Kidney Pond and Nesowadnehunk Field, you get a better view of the whole east face of the mountain with its two peaks. Doubletop Mountain is one of those mountains that are so picture perfect they demand to be climbed. And the view from the peaks rewards the work and fulfills all expectations.

MILES AND DIRECTIONS

0.0 Start from the sign-in box next to the bridge over Nesowadnehunk Stream.

0.3 The trail crosses the bridge and turns left, following the stream through the campground. At the end of the campground, the woods road becomes a trail.

1.8 The trail climbs gently, then descends to ford Doubletop Stream.

2.5 The trail begins climbing steeply immediately across Doubletop Stream. When the trail begins to level out, there's an old sign informing hikers that there's another 1.0 mile to the North Peak.

3.4 The trail climbs gently along the summit ridge, then climbs steeply to North Peak. The sign for the peak is 20 feet below the rock summit.

3.8 The trail drops off North Peak and crosses the mostly open saddle between the two peaks along cliff tops with views across Nesowadnehunk Valley. South Peak is a rocky projection that hangs off the south end of the summit ridge. To complete the hike, return the way you came back toward the trailhead. **OPTION:** The Doubletop Mountain Trail continues by dropping very steeply off the west side of the summit ridge, reaching Kidney Pond in 4.3 miles. You could use this trail to cross over the mountain and make the hike an 8.1-mile shuttle hike.

7.6 Arrive back at the trailhead.

13. NORTH BROTHER

WHY GO?
The view from the rocky dome on the North Brother's summit is the best view in Maine. To get there, you follow the Marston Trail. There are three distinct climbs on the hike; the second one past the pond is the most challenging. The upper trail is very eroded and overgrown.

THE RUN DOWN

Start: From the Marston Trailhead at the east end of the parking area.

Elevation gain: 3,201 feet.

Distance: 9.0 miles out and back

Hiking time: 5–6 hours.

Difficulty: Most strenuous.

Seasons: June–Sept are best.

Trail surface: Woodland path.

Nearest town: Millinocket.

Other users: None.

Water availability: Roaring Brook at mile 1.6.

Other maps: *DeLorme's The Maine Atlas and Gazetteer* map 50.

Nat Geo TOPO! Map (USGS): Doubletop and Katahdin.

Nat Geo Trails Illustrated Map: Baxter State Park.

FINDING THE TRAILHEAD

From the Togue Pond Gate, drive 13.4 miles. The Marston Trailhead parking is on the right 0.1 mile before the Slide Dam picnic area. The trailhead is at the east end of the parking area.
Trailhead GPS: N45° 56.357' / W69° 02.480'.

WHAT TO SEE
The Marston Trail was built in the 1950s by a group of explorer scouts led by James and Philip Marston. The trail leaves the parking area and crosses through mature hardwoods to a tumbling stream. The trail climbs steadily along the stream. As you climb, the trail crosses and recrosses several gullies and rills.

The best view in Baxter: Katahdin from North Brother's summit

Beyond the junction with the south end of the Mount Coe Trail, the trail climbs gently to a small pond nestled in a cirque. Across the pond, water loudly streams down faces of bare rock. The trail skirts the pond to the south and switchbacks up to the top of the cirque's headwall. This is the steepest section of the hike. There's a small overlook with views of the pond far below and the mountains to the south and west.

Above the headwall, the trail climbs more gently through spruce to the wide valley between North and South Brothers. Past the north end of the Mount Coe Trail, you descend slightly to the wet, sandy beginning of a stream that drains into The Klondike. The trail begins to climb gently, then more steeply. This section of trail is very eroded and overhung with foliage. You may begin to wonder if you've wandered off trail and onto a streambed. The occasional, faded blue blaze keeps you going. Then, you break out of the trees and the crenellated summit is right there above you. To get here, you've climbed 3,000 feet.

Most people who visit Baxter climb Katahdin to say they have and for the magnificent view. Arguably, views of Katahdin are more spectacular than those from it. And the view of Katahdin from the North Brother is the best. You can see Davis

Pond hanging high in the Northwest Basin. The bare dome of the Northwest Plateau dominates the middle view. Next to it, and slightly farther off, are the peaks surrounding the Great Basin: Pamola Peak, Chimney Peak, the Knife Edge, and Baxter Peak—all are outlined against the sky. Turning, you see The Owl, Barren Mountain, South Brother, and Mount Coe. Turning more, you see Doubletop and the Kettle Mountains in the hazy distance, then Center Mountain, Fort Mountain, and all the remote mountains around Russell Pond.

The best part is that you'll likely have North Brother to yourself. No one else will be there to judge your open-mouthed stare.

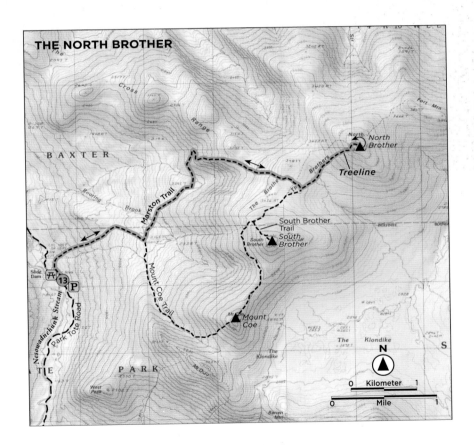

Katahdin and Barren Mountain from near North Brother's summit

MILES AND DIRECTIONS

0.0   Start from the Marston Trailhead at the east end of the parking area.

0.3   The trail crosses relatively level ground to stream, then begins to climb.

1.3   Climb steadily to junction with the Mount Coe Trail. Bear left, staying on the Marston Trail.

2.0   Climb gently to a shallow pond nestled against a shoulder of the mountain.

2.8   The trail goes around the pond, then climbs steeply to an overlook.

3.6   The trail climbs more gently to a junction with the other end of the Mount Coe Trail. Continue straight ahead on the Marston Trail.

4.1   The trail crosses a saddle, then climbs steeply up the overgrown and eroded trail to tree line.

4.5   The trail crosses through stunted trees and boulders to the summit. To complete the hike, return the way you came.

9.0   Arrive back at the trailhead.

14. MOUNT COE

WHY GO?

Mount Coe is a spruce-covered dome west of The Klondike. It's a small, open summit, offering spectacular views in every direction. The Mount Coe Trail follows a small stream up the steep valley between Mounts Coe and O-J-I. Climbing the huge slide on the face of Mount Coe is straightforward, unless you are afraid of heights. This hike includes nearby South Brother, which has similar views from its wide, rocky summit.

THE RUN DOWN

Start: From the Marston Trailhead at the east end of the parking area.

Elevation gain: 3,327 feet.

Distance: 9.0 miles lollipop.

Hiking time: 6–8 hours.

Difficulty: Most strenuous.

Seasons: June–Oct are best.

Trail surface: Woodland path and granite bedrock.

Nearest town: Millinocket.

Other users: None.

Water availability: The Mount Coe Trail follows a reliable stream from the Marston Trail to the rock slide.

Other maps: *DeLorme's The Maine Atlas and Gazetteer* map 50.

Nat Geo TOPO! Map (USGS): Doubletop Mountain.

Nat Geo Trails Illustrated Map: Baxter State Park.

FINDING THE TRAILHEAD

From the Togue Pond Gate, drive 13.4 miles. The Marston Trailhead parking is on the right 0.1 mile before the Slide Dam picnic area. The trailhead is at the east end of the parking area.

Trailhead GPS: N45° 56.357' / W69° 02.480'.

WHAT TO SEE

The west side of The Klondike is lined with rugged mountains: Mounts O-J-I, Coe, and North and South Brothers. All four are connected by trails, but it's not recommended to climb more than two at a time. They're just too challenging. This hike climbs Mount Coe and then South Brother, making a manageable 9-mile hike. It's possible to hike Mount Coe as a 6-mile out-and-back, but that requires descending the slide—something not recommended.

Mount Coe from Mount O-J-I

The Marston Trail climbs steadily, then steeply to the Mount Coe Trail. The Mount Coe Trail follows a small stream up the steep, narrow valley between Mounts O-J-I and Coe. The rocky spine of O-J-I's summit ridge dominates your view. As you climb, the way becomes rougher, the mossy woods giving way to powdered granite chock-full of irregular boulders.

The trail turns north and climbs straight up the huge slide that dominates the face of Mount Coe. As you ascend the slide, it becomes steeper and smoother. The view is incredible, so long as you are not afraid of heights. Other slide trails in Baxter have been rerouted for safety: Abol, O-J-I, and Dudley.

From the top of the slide, it's an easy climb through stunted spruce to the summit. You have a spectacular 360 degree view and a great spot for lunch. The trail continues north, descending into the wide notch between Mount Coe and South Brother. You slab around South Brother to the west, where a short, steep side trail climbs to the wide summit.

The Mount Coe Trail ends at the Marston Trail. You can turn right and hike nearly a mile to North Brother, or save that mountain for another day. The descent

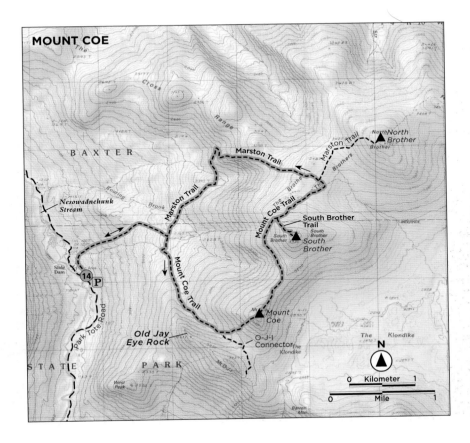

on the Marston Trail is extremely steep in places. The trail passes a small, rocky pond ringed by alders and skeletal trees tucked into a cirque.

When you get back to the trailhead, having climbed and then descended nearly 3,400 knee-pounding feet, you'll be ready for a soak in Nesowadnehunk Stream at nearby Ledge Falls.

MILES AND DIRECTIONS

0.0   Start from the Marston Trailhead at the north end of the parking area.

1.3   The trail climbs steeply to the Mount Coe Trail. Turn right onto Mount Coe Trail.

2.1   The trail climbs steadily alongside a small stream to the base of a large slide.

2.8   The trail climbs the slide. Be sure to follow the blazes. This is a potentially dangerous section of trail. At the top of the slide, the trail reenters the forest.

The Brothers from Mount Coe's summit

3.0   Reach Mount Coe's small, open summit. **OPTION:** You can return the way you came. Remember descending the slide is going to be more difficult and more dangerous than climbing it.

4.1   The trail descends off Mount Coe and slabs around the west side of the South Brother. Turn right onto the South Brother Trail.

4.4   Reach the wide, open summit of South Brother. To continue the hike, return to the Mount Coe Trail.

4.7   Turn right back onto the Mount Coe Trail.

5.3   The Mount Coe Trail ends at the Marston Trail. Turn left to return to the trailhead. **OPTION:** You can turn right and hike 0.8 mile to the summit of North Brother.

7.0   The trail descends very steeply to a small pond.

7.7   Pass the Mount Coe Trail.

9.0   Arrive back at the trailhead.

15. MOUNT O-J-I

WHY GO?

Mount O-J-I offers fine views from all along its summit ridge, from Old Jay Eye Rock at the west end where the trail ascends to the east across the summit. Before reaching the summit ridge, the trail passes West Peak with fine views. The new trail to the summit ridge makes one of the more interesting climbs in Baxter. It's an exhilarating hike, the easiest of the four Katahdinauguoh mountains.

THE RUN DOWN

Start: From the O-J-I Trailhead at the north end of the parking area.

Elevation gain: 2,658 feet.

Distance: 8.9 miles out and back.

Hiking time: 5–7 hours.

Difficulty: Most strenuous.

Seasons: June–Oct are best.

Trail surface: Woodland path.

Nearest town: Millinocket.

Other users: None.

Water availability: Small spring at mile 0.7.

Other maps: *DeLorme's The Maine Atlas and Gazetteer* map 50.

Nat Geo TOPO! Map (USGS): Doubletop Mountain.

Nat Geo Trails Illustrated Map: Baxter State Park.

FINDING THE TRAILHEAD

From the Togue Pond Gate, drive 10.3 miles on the Park Tote Road. The trailhead is on the left 0.2 mile past the Daicey Pond Road.
Trailhead GPS: N45° 54.202' / W69° 02.226'.

WHAT TO SEE

The O-J-I Trail used to go straight up one of several slides to the summit ridge. Park officials decided to reroute the trail for safety reasons—the O-J-I slides are unstable. In fact, the mountain's name comes from the shape of the three largest slides. Today, though, the slides no longer look the letters they're named for. They've grown and almost merged into one giant slide.

The trail now climbs to the base of the mountain, then slabs northwest, climbing into the saddle between Mount O-J-I and West Peak. A side trail climbs 0.3 mile to the top of West Peak. The mostly open summit offers a fine panoramic view.

Past the side trail to West Peak, the O-J-I Trail climbs steeply through a thick, rocky forest. The ridge narrows and steepens as you climb. Eventually, you reach the

Mount O-J-I's summit

base of Old Jay Eye Rock. The trail squeezes through a crack in the rock and climbs to its open, precipitous summit. The Nesowadnehunk Stream winds far below among steep, granite mountains.

The trail continues to the east, climbing along the mostly open summit ridge. The summit itself is hidden in a dense, stunted forest. Beyond the summit, the trail descends gently to an overlook with a view of Katahdin across The Klondike. The high cliffs of the Northwest Basin are visible behind the wide arm of Katahdin. Mount Coe dominates the view to the north, blocking The Brothers entirely. The huge slide on its face looks like a serious wound that refuses to heal.

The trail does continue down into the notch between Mounts O-J-I and Coe, where it ends at the Mount Coe Trail. It's therefore possible to combine the two mountains into one hike.

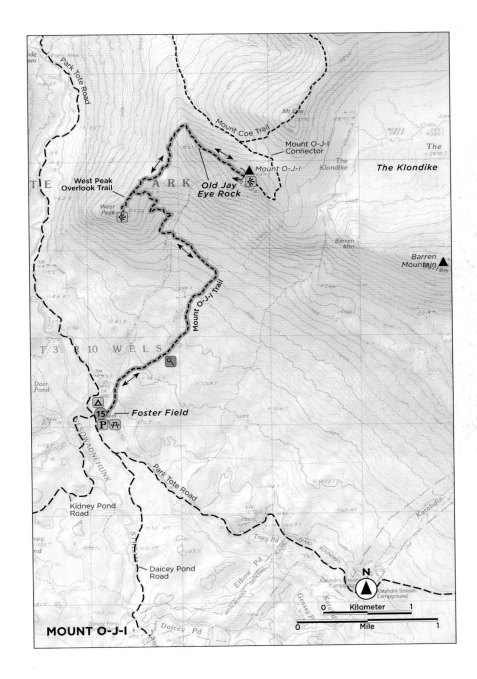

Park Tote Road

Mount Coe Trail

Mount O-J-I
Connector

The
Klondike

The Klondike

▲ Mount O-J-I

Old Jay
Eye Rock

West Peak
Overlook Trail

West
Peak

Barren
Mtn

Barren
Mountain ▲

Mount O-J-I Trail

Deer
Pond

15

P 🏕

Foster Field

Park Tote Road

Kidney Pond
Road

Daicey Pond
Road

Daicey Pd

Tracy Pd

Katahdin Stream
Campground

N

0   Kilometer   1

0   Mile   1

MOUNT O-J-I

Looking west along Mount O-J-I's summit ridge

MILES AND DIRECTIONS

0.0   Start from the Mount O-J-I Trailhead at the north end of the parking area.

0.7   The trail passes through a wet area to a small spring.

2.7   The trail climbs to the saddle between Mount O-J-I and West Peak. Turn left onto the West Peak Overlook Trail.

3.0   Arrive at the overlook with fine views in every direction. To continue the hike, return to the Mount O-J-I Trail.

3.3   Go straight onto the Mount O-J-I Trail.

4.2   The trail crosses the saddle, then begins to climb steeply to Old Jay Eye Rock.

4.6   The trail climbs along a mostly open ridge to the wooded summit.

4.7   Arrive at an overlook with fine views in every direction. To complete the hike, return the way you came.

8.9   Arrive back at the trailhead.

16. SLAUGHTER POND

WHY GO?

Slaughter Pond is a long, narrow lake fast against the rocky spine that connects Bean Hole and Moose Mountains. To get there, you hike past Draper Pond, cross Slaughter Brook, loop around Deer Pond, and hike through a beautiful, hardwood forest. There's a small hill at the beginning of the hike; the rest is flat. This hike is good for seeing wildlife. The last 0.2 mile is out of Baxter State Park in a Nature Conservancy preserve.

THE RUN DOWN

Start: From the Doubletop Mountain Trailhead at the northeast end of the Kidney Pond day-use parking area.

Elevation gain: 655 feet.

Distance: 6.6 miles out and back.

Hiking time: About 4 hours.

Difficulty: Moderate.

Seasons: May–Oct are best.

Trail surface: Woodland path.

Nearest town: Millinocket.

Other users: None.

Water availability: Draper Pond and Slaughter Pond.

Other maps: *DeLorme's The Maine Atlas and Gazetteer* map 50.

Nat Geo TOPO! Map (USGS): Doubletop Mountain.

Nat Geo Trails Illustrated Map: Baxter State Park.

FINDING THE TRAILHEAD

 From the Togue Pond Gate, drive 10.4 miles. Turn left onto the Kidney Pond Road. Drive 1.2 miles to the day-use parking at the end of the road. The trailhead is at the southeast end of the parking area.

Trailhead GPS: N45° 53.647' / W69° 02.919'.

WHAT TO SEE

Slaughter Pond sits up against the crenelated ridge that links Bean Hole Mountain to Moose Mountain. Moose Mountain is one of those whose name was changed in 1999 to remove the word "squaw" from Maine place-names. Some maps refer to it as Moose's Bosom Mountain, which is closer to the original name. From the Kidney Pond area, this mountain is the rounded hump west of pointy Doubletop Mountain. Moose Mountain and Slaughter Pond are outside Baxter State Park in Nature Conservancy land, but the trail from Baxter is the only access to the pond. It's one of the most scenic ponds in the region.

Slaughter Pond from the end of the trail

Slaughter Pond was so named to remember a winter moose hunt in the mid-1800s. Hunters chased a group of moose out onto the pond. The moose were unable to flee across the slippery ice and the hunters killed thirteen of them. Today, there are several likely places to see moose along this hike, especially the swampy sections of Slaughter Brook near the pond and around Deer Pond.

The hike follows Doubletop Mountain Trail over a rocky hill. Near the top of the hill is the side trail down to Draper Pond. There's a rental canoe. It's a pretty pond with a fine view of Mount O-J-I from the shore. Watch for ducks and wildlife in the pond. Past Draper Pond, Doubletop Mountain Trail descends gently through the mossy, stony, evergreen forest west of Rocky Pond.

You have to cross Slaughter Brook on fallen logs. This section is often wet and muddy. Just upstream from the crossing is a beaver dam. The trail follows the stream toward Deer Pond. Watch for moose and beaver. From the blueberry bushes along the shore of Deer Pond, you have a fine view of Doubletop Mountain. Again, be on the lookout for wildlife.

Past Deer Pond, you reach a junction. To the right, Slaughter Pond Trail loops around Draper Pond and ends at Kidney Pond Road in 0.9 mile. To the left, the trail is both Slaughter Pond and Doubletop Mountain Trails. Turn left and skirt the north shore of Deer Pond.

BLOWDOWNS

Where the Doubletop Mountain Trail climbs away from Deer Pond, you pass through a huge blowdown. On July 19, 2013, a severe storm system passed through Baxter State Park, producing microbursts and a small tornado. This blowdown and one farther along the hike were the results of that storm. Damage from the storm can also be seen near the beginning of Horse Mountain Trail, along the Tote Road east of Trout Brook Farm, along the Kidney Pond Road north of Nesowadnehunk Stream, and along Webster Stream on the Freezeout Trail.

I was hiking with my son on the day of the storm. We were between the two blowdowns on the hike to Slaughter Pond when they happened. The wind was strong enough to bend all the trees over thirty degrees and as loud as a freight trail. Rain poured down in sheets. We were lucky to make it to Kidney Pond in one piece.

Slaughter Pond is almost due west with very little up and down. You hike through a mostly hardwood forest. As you near Slaughter Pond, you'll notice a large swampy area south of the trail. This is Slaughter Brook.

Just before you reach the pond, you pass through what appears to be a canoe parking lot. As many as forty canoes are leaning against trees or sitting on the ground. All the canoes are a testament to the quality of fishing and scenery at Slaughter Pond.

Doubletop Mountain from Deer Pond. Notice the moose standing in the pond where Slaughter Brook flows in

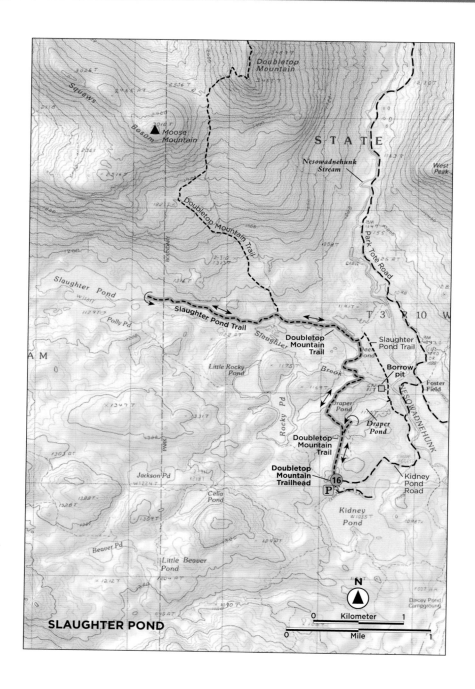

SLAUGHTER POND

The trail ends at the narrow east end of the pond where the stream flows out. To the south, a low rocky hill separates Slaughter and Polly Ponds. To the north is the ridge that runs from Bean Hole Mountain to Moose Mountain. Along the ridge are several rocky caps. Because the pond is outside Baxter State Park, there's no rental canoe here.

MILES AND DIRECTIONS

0.0 Start from the Doubletop Mountain Trailhead at the northwest end of the Kidney Pond day-use parking area. **OPTION:** You can begin the hike at the Slaughter Pond Trailhead 0.9 mile northeast on Kidney Pond Road, just before the bridge over Nesowadnehunk Stream. This option is 0.9 mile shorter each way, but much less scenic and with fewer opportunities to see wildlife.

0.4 Doubletop Mountain Trail climbs gently to Draper Pond Trail. Turn right.

0.5 Draper Pond Trail descends to the southwest end of Draper Pond, where there's a rental canoe. To continue the hike, return to Doubletop Mountain Trail.

0.6 Turn right onto Doubletop Mountain Trail.

1.1 The trail crosses a rocky hill, then descends to cross Slaughter Brook.

1.4 The trail parallels Slaughter Brook to Deer Pond.

1.7 The trail loops around Deer Pond to the west to a junction with Slaughter Pond Trail. Turn left.

2.3 Go straight, staying on Slaughter Pond Trail.

3.1 The trail crosses out of Baxter State Park and into Nature Conservancy land.

3.3 The trail ends at the east end of Slaughter Pond. To complete the hike, return the way you came.

6.6 Arrive back at the trailhead.

17. ROCKY PONDS

WHY GO?

The Rocky Ponds lie south of Doubletop Mountain, an easy hike from Kidney Pond. From the shore of each pond, you have fine views of Doubletop Mountain and Mount O-J-I. The trail to and between the ponds passes through a spruce forest that is among the mossiest in Maine. Both ponds have rental canoes.

THE RUN DOWN

Start: From the Sentinel Link Trailhead at the southeast end of the parking area.

Elevation gain: 233 feet.

Distance: 2.4 miles out and back.

Hiking time: 1–2 hours.

Difficulty: Easy.

Seasons: May–Oct are best.

Trail surface: Woodland path.

Nearest town: Millinocket.

Other users: None.

Water availability: None.

Other maps: *DeLorme's The Maine Atlas and Gazetteer* map 50.

Nat Geo TOPO! Map (USGS): Doubletop Mountain.

Nat Geo Trails Illustrated Map: Baxter State Park.

FINDING THE TRAILHEAD

 From the Togue Pond Gate, drive 10.4 miles. Turn left onto the Kidney Pond Road. Drive 1.2 miles to the day-use parking at the end of the road. The trailhead is at the southeast end of the parking area.

Trailhead GPS: N45° 53.621' / W69° 02.931'.

WHAT TO SEE

In the wide Nesowadnehunk Valley, south of Doubletop Mountain, is a collection of twenty or so ponds. Many of the ponds have trails to them and rental canoes on their shores. Each pond is unique in its own way and worth visiting. The ponds are good places to see moose and other wildlife, especially early in the morning or at sunset.

The Rocky Ponds are an easy hike from Kidney Pond. The trail winds through a rocky, spruce forest. It may be the mossiest place in Maine. After a rain, the forest

Mossy trail between the two Rocky Ponds

glows in emerald glory. The section of trail between the two ponds is especially mossy. In spring, wildflowers are splashed across the forest floor.

Both Rocky Ponds have a park rental canoe—the ranger at Kidney Pond collects fees and give out the keys. From the shore and on the water, you have a fine view of Doubletop and Moose Mountains to the north. They're an interesting pair; the one a rounded hump, the other a sharp cone. To the east, you have a good view of Mount O-J-I and its slide-scarred face.

The ponds themselves are irregular drops in the forest, shallow with boulders breaking the surface here and there. A quiet and picturesque spot surrounded by so much wilderness.

Little Rocky Pond

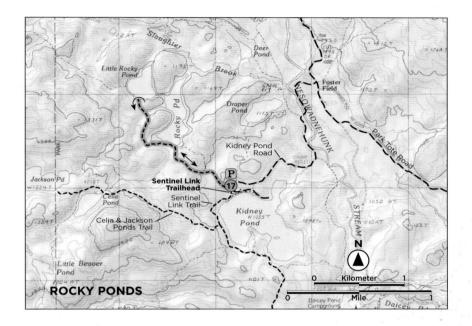

ROCKY PONDS

MILES AND DIRECTIONS

0.0 Start from the Sentinel Link Trailhead at the southeast end of the day-use parking area. In 200 feet, turn right onto the Rocky Ponds Trail.

0.6 Reach the south shore of Rocky Pond. The trail continues west along the shore of the pond.

1.2 The trail climbs over a small hill and ends at the south shore of Little Rocky Pond. To complete the hike, return the way you came.

2.4 Arrive back at the trailhead.

18. CELIA & JACKSON PONDS

WHY GO?

The hike follows the rocky east shore of Kidney Pond to Jackson Landing. From there, you hike over a small hill to marsh-fringed Celia Pond. The trail continues out of Baxter State Park to the larger Jackson Pond. Across Jackson Pond, Doubletop and Moose Mountains can be seen. To the east, you can see Mount O-J-I.

THE RUN DOWN

Start: From the Kidney Pond Area Trailhead at the east end of the day-use parking area at the end of Kidney Pond Road.

Elevation gain: 360 feet.

Distance: 3.2 miles out and back.

Hiking time: About 2 hours.

Difficulty: Easy.

Seasons: May–Oct are best.

Trail surface: Woodland path.

Nearest town: Millinocket.

Other users: None.

Water availability: Kidney Pond and Jackson Pond.

Other maps: *DeLorme's The Maine Atlas and Gazetteer* map 50.

Nat Geo TOPO! Map (USGS): Doubletop Mountain.

Nat Geo Trails Illustrated Map: Baxter State Park.

FINDING THE TRAILHEAD

 From the Togue Pond Gate, drive 10.4 miles. Turn left onto the Kidney Pond Road. Drive 1.2 miles to the day-use parking at the end of the road. The trailhead is at the southeast end of the parking area.

Trailhead GPS: N45° 53.621' / W69° 02.931'.

WHAT TO SEE

The Sentinel Link Trail, along the south shore of Kidney Pond, offers classic views of Katahdin and its attendant peaks. Look for loons and ducks hanging out in the pond with canoes and kayaks. At Jackson Landing, Celia & Jackson Ponds Trail climbs west away from Kidney Pond. The trail passes through a forest of spruce and moss-covered boulders. Small wildflowers like wood sorrel grow from the moss. Drifts of needles add orange to the emerald scene. The trail passes one particularly large, cabin-sized boulder.

Moose Mountain and Doubletop
Mountain from Jackson Pond

Celia Pond

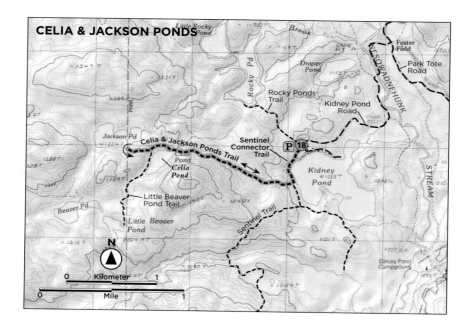

The trail passes out of the moss forest and slabs around a rocky hill before reaching Celia Pond. Around the pond, the boulders are smaller and the moss less lush. Maybe the weather created by Katahdin that washes across Kidney Pond and keeps the forest cool and damp can't reach quite this far.

Unlike most of the ponds in the Kidney Pond area, Celia Pond is marsh-fringed. Moss-covered rocks stop short of the shore, where bushes and reeds abound. Along the north shore, the trail passes a huge pile of boulders covered with moss and adventurous trees.

Jackson Pond is more akin to the nearby Rocky Ponds. Rocks and boulders are pushed against its shore, moved outward by the season's freeze–thaw cycle. Evergreens crowd the pond. In the distance, jagged mountains mark the sky. The untrailed hump of Moose Mountain reclines next to the rocky pyramid of Doubletop Mountain. Farther east, you can see Mount O-J-I. Its many slides of stained granite no longer spell out its name, having merged together over time.

Jackson and Celia Ponds have rental canoes.

oknlkgg nb njohnni bnlj

MILES AND DIRECTIONS

0.0 Start from the Kidney Pond Area Trailhead at the southwest end of the day-use parking area.

0.3 Follow the Sentinel Connector Trail along the south shore of Kidney Pond to Jackson Landing. Turn right onto Celia & Jackson Ponds Trail.

0.6 The trail climbs gently through a forest of spruce and moss-covered boulders, then slabs around a rocky hill.

1.2 Reach the shore of Celia Pond.

1.4 The trail follows the east shore of Celia Pond. Pass the Little Beaver Pond Trail.

1.6 Reach the south shore of Jackson Pond. To complete the hike, return the way you came.

3.2 Arrive back at the trailhead.

19. SENTINEL MOUNTAIN

WHY GO?

Sentinel Mountain is a rocky ridge that rises more than 1,000 feet above the West Branch of the Penobscot River in the southwest corner of Baxter. The hike passes through areas of forest and bog before climbing to the summit ridge. The trail loops around the summit, crossing open bedrock and patches of forest and blueberries. There are several viewpoints along the way.

THE RUN DOWN

Start: From the Sentinel Link Trailhead at the southeast end of the day-use parking area.

Elevation gain: 1,134 feet.

Distance: 5.6 miles out and back.

Hiking time: About 4 hours.

Difficulty: Moderate.

Seasons: May–Oct are best.

Trail surface: Woodland path.

Nearest town: Millinocket.

Other users: None.

Water availability: None.

Other maps: *DeLorme's The Maine Atlas and Gazetteer* map 50.

Nat Geo TOPO! Map (USGS): Doubletop Mountain and Rainbow Lake East.

Nat Geo Trails Illustrated Map: Baxter State Park.

FINDING THE TRAILHEAD

From the Togue Pond Gate, drive 10.4 miles. Turn left onto the Kidney Pond Road. Drive 1.2 miles to the day-use parking at the end of the road. The trailhead is at the southeast end of the parking area.

Trailhead GPS: N45° 53.621' / W69° 02.931'.

WHAT TO SEE

Sentinel Mountain, or just The Sentinel, rises more than 1,000 feet above the West Branch of the Penobscot River. The Indians named the mountain for the way it seems to guard Katahdin and its attendant mountains from the prying eyes of those on and along the river. From the north, in Baxter, it's an almost unnoticeable bump on the landscape. Don't let that fool you. For many Mainers, this unassuming mountain is one of their favorites.

The trailhead is south from Kidney Pond through a rolling, hardwood forest. You descend gently to Beaver Brook and the bogs along its course. Across the stream, the

Along the loop trail on Sentinel Mountain's summit.

forest becomes mostly evergreens, as you climb gently toward Sentinel Mountain. As the trail nears the mountain, it begins climbing a rocky canyon with a small stream tumbling through it. The trail climbs above the stream, where a group of large boulders cap the ridge. The trail climbs through a gap in the rock, like a staircase to the summit.

The trail loops around the summit over bare granite, among blueberries, and through dense stands of spruce and birch. Here and there the summit opens. As you work your way around the summit, you have views of Katahdin and Mount O-J-I, Doubletop and Moose Mountains, and finally the West Branch. The face of Sentinel Mountain facing the river is more open and rocky. A good place to sit and gorge on blueberries like a bear and contemplate the world below.

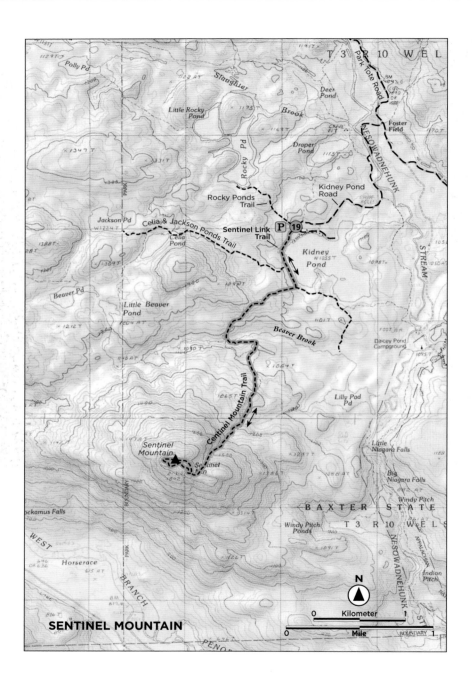

SENTINEL MOUNTAIN

The rocky gateway to Sentinel Mountain's summit

MILES AND DIRECTIONS

0.0 Start from the Sentinel Link Trailhead at the southeast end of the day-use parking area.

0.3 Almost immediately pass the Rocky Ponds Trail, the Kidney Stone (a large erratic boulder to the left of the trail), and the Celia & Jackson Ponds Trail.

0.5 Turn right onto the Sentinel Mountain Trail.

1.2 Cross Beaver Brook.

2.5 Climb gently, then steadily, to a fork on the east end of Sentinel Mountain's summit ridge. Turn right.

3.1 The trail loops around the summit with fine views in every direction—and lots of blueberries. Arrive back at the fork. Descend the way you came to return to the trailhead.

5.6 Arrive back at the trailhead.

20. LILY PAD POND

WHY GO?
Lily Pad Pond rests against the flank of Sentinel Mountain. From the small, shallow pond, you have spectacular views of the mountains from Moose Mountain to Katahdin. Beaver Brook and Lily Pad Pond offer good wildlife viewing. Windy Pitch Pond Trail begins on the south shore of Lily Pad Pond. The trail crosses a small hill, then reaches Little and Big Niagara Falls. Beyond the falls, the trail crosses a mossy forest to Windy Pitch Pond.

THE RUN DOWN

Start: From the Sentinel Link Trailhead at the southeast end of the day-use parking area.

Elevation gain: 617 feet.

Distance: 6.2 miles out and back.

Hiking time: 1–2 hours.

Difficulty: Easy.

Seasons: May–Oct are best.

Trail surface: Woodland path and flat water canoeing.

Nearest town: Millinocket.

Other users: None.

Water availability: Kidney Pond and Nesowadnehunk Stream.

Other maps: *DeLorme's The Maine Atlas and Gazetteer* map 50.

Nat Geo TOPO! Map (USGS): Doubletop Mountain.

Nat Geo Trails Illustrated Map: Baxter State Park.

FINDING THE TRAILHEAD

From the Togue Pond Gate, drive 10.4 miles. Turn left onto the Kidney Pond Road. Drive 1.2 miles to the day-use parking at the end of the road. The trailhead is at the southeast end of the parking area.

Trailhead GPS: N45° 53.621' / W69° 02.931'.

WHAT TO SEE
Lily Pad Pond is little more than a wide spot in Beaver Brook just before it empties into Nesowadnehunk Stream. The pond is ringed by marsh, densely packed laurel and cranberry bushes with the occasional spruce or larch standing like sentries. Alders grow as close as they dare, creeping in from along Nesowadnehunk Stream. It's a pretty spot where you might see moose or ducks. To the west, rises the rounded hump of Sentinel Mountain—its crown showing bald spots here and there. To the north, from the west all the way around to the east, is a line of great mountains: Moose and Doubletop Mountains, the Nesowadnehunk Valley, Western Peak and

The spectacular line of mountains
seen from Lily Pad Pond

Mount O-J-I with Mount Coe peeking out from behind, the long ridge of Barren Mountain, and the huge mass of Katahdin from the Northwest Plateau to the Knife Edge—a magnificent view.

To get there, you follow the Sentinel Link Trail along the south shore of Kidney Pond. Take the side trail to Colt Point, which sits in the bend of the Kidney Pond. From its rocky shore, you have fine views of the entire pond and the mountains beyond. You can rent a canoe at Kidney Pond campground and paddle down the pond to Lily Pad Landing, saving almost a mile of walking.

The Lily Pad Pond Trail is less mossy than many of the other trails that lead south from Kidney Pond, but it's a pleasant walk. The trail ends with a boardwalk through an alder break to Beaver Brook. The brook flows from the Beaver Ponds just outside the park southwest of Celia & Jackson Ponds. Upstream from the trail's end, the brook tumbles out of the woods into a wet meadow. Early in the summer, you can paddle its sinuous course to the woods. Downstream, Beaver Brook widens, hemmed in by dense bushes. Pitcher plants, sundews, cotton grass, and all manner of bog plants grow among the bushes on the dense mat of moss. Paddle downstream and into Lily Pad Pond. The view of the mountains opens up as you put distance between yourself and land dry enough to support forest.

To continue the hike, paddle to the east end of the pond where it narrows to a rock-filled stream. The take out is a flat, open area just beyond where the outlet stream disappears into rock-choked alders.

The Windy Pitch Pond Trail enters the woods and climbs a small, rocky hill. You can hear the falls on Nesowadnehunk Stream. You drop down off the hill to Little Niagara Falls. Short, unmarked side trails lead to both the top and base of the falls. The view of the falls from its base is far superior to the view you get from the Appalachian Trail on the other side of the stream.

A short distance farther, you come to a short side trail that leads to the top of Big Niagara Falls. An unmarked, but well-worn trail continues down to the base of the falls. Again, the view from this vantage is better than from the other side of the stream.

The Windy Pitch Pond Trail continues another half mile to its namesake pond. This small pond is surrounded by a dense forest. Exposed rock is visible on the steep slopes south and west of the pond. There's a rental canoe on the north shore where the trail ends.

This is very nearly a perfect hike with beautiful woods, pretty ponds, waterfalls, spectacular views, wildlife, and solitude. This is a hike to take your time with. Make it last the whole day and really explore.

Looking across Lily Pad Pond
from the take ou

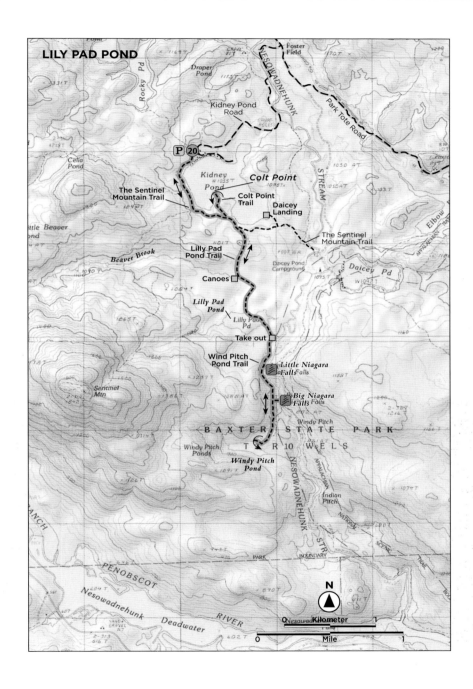

LILY PAD POND

Rocky Pd
Draper Pond
NESOWADNEHUNK STREAM
Foster Field
Park Tote Road
Kidney Pond Road
Celia Pond
P 20
Kidney Pond
Colt Point
The Sentinel Mountain Trail
Colt Point Trail
Daicey Landing
The Sentinel Mountain Trail
Little Beaver Pond
Beaver Brook
Lilly Pad Pond Trail
Canoes
Daicey Pond Campground
Daicey Pd
Lilly Pad Pond
Lilly Pad Pd
Take out
Wind Pitch Pond Trail
Little Niagara Falls
Sentinel Mtn
Big Niagara Falls
B A X T E R S T A T E P A R K
T R 10 W E L S
Windy Pitch Ponds
Windy Pitch Pond
NESOWADNEHUNK STREAM
Indian Pitch
PENOBSCOT BRANCH
Nesowadnehunk
Deadwater RIVER
PARK BOUNDARY

N

0 Kilometer 1
0 Mile 1

MILES AND DIRECTIONS

0.0 Start from the Sentinel Link Trailhead at the southeast end of the day-use parking area.

0.1 Pass the Rocky Ponds Trail and the Kidney Stone—a large erratic boulder to the left of the trail.

0.3 Pass the Celia & Jackson Ponds Trail.

0.5 Continue straight ahead along the south shore of Kidney Pond onto the Sentinel Mountain Trail.

0.7 Turn left onto the Colt Point Trail.

0.9 Arrive at Colt Point. To continue the hike, return to the Sentinel Mountain Trail.

1.1 Turn left onto the Sentinel Mountain Trail.

1.3 Turn right onto the Lily Pad Pond Trail.

1.6 The trail emerges from the woods and crosses a marshy area on bog boards, ending at Beaver Brook. Unlock your canoe and paddle downstream, east to the left.

2.0 Beaver Brook opens into Lily Pad Pond.

2.2 Cross Lily Pad Pond to the southeast. The landing is beyond the rocks at the mouth of the outlet stream. Be sure to pull your canoe all the way out of the water before leaving it. Windy Pitch Pond Trail is to the south.

2.5 The trail crosses a small hill and reaches Little Niagara Falls. There are unmarked side trails to both the top and base of the falls.

2.8 Turn left onto the side trail to Big Niagara Falls.

3.0 The trail reaches the top of the falls and continues down the rocky slope to the base of the falls. To continue the hike, return to Windy Pitch Pond Trail.

3.2 Turn left onto Windy Pitch Pond Trail.

3.5 The trail ends on the north shore of Windy Pitch Pond at the rental canoe. To complete the hike, return the way you came.

6.2 Arrive back at the trailhead.

21. NIAGARA FALLS

WHY GO?

Big and Little Niagara Falls on Nesowadnehunk Stream are two of Baxter State Park's wilder falls. They're also among the most accessible. The short hike along the southbound Appalachian Trail is an easy walk on a section of wide trail through an evergreen forest full of rocks and moss. The hike first visits the Toll Dam, a remnant of Nesowadnehunk Stream's historic log drives. Below the dam are the two falls. At each falls are large areas of granite that you can climb on and explore, offering different views of each falls.

THE RUN DOWN

Start: From the day-use parking area where the Appalachian Trail crosses the Daicey Pond Road. The hike follows the southbound AT.

Elevation gain: 361 feet, mostly on the return hike.

Distance: 3.0 miles out and back.

Hiking time: 2–3 hours.

Difficulty: Easy.

Seasons: June–Sept are best.

Trail surface: Woodland path.

Nearest town: Millinocket.

Other users: None.

Water availability: Nesowadnehunk Stream at the Toll Dam.

Other maps: *DeLorme's The Maine Atlas and Gazetteer* map 50.

Nat Geo TOPO! Map (USGS): Doubletop Mountain and Rainbow Lake East.

Nat Geo Trails Illustrated Map: Baxter State Park.

FINDING THE TRAILHEAD

From the south entrance of Baxter State Park at Togue Pond Gate, drive 10.1 miles on the Tote Road. Turn left onto the Daicey Pond Road at the sign for Daicey Pond. Drive 1.5 miles. The day-use parking is on the right where the Appalachian Trail crosses the road. The hike follows the southbound AT.
Trailhead GPS: N45° 52.940' / W69° 01.909'.

WHAT TO SEE

Nesowadnehunk Stream runs for 17 miles from Little Nesowadnehunk Lake just west of Baxter State Park south to the Penobscot River. The first 5.0 miles from the lake to Nesowadnehunk Field drops very little. Between Nesowadnehunk Field and the Kidney Pond Road, the stream is much wilder, dropping in a series of falls and rapids, including Ledge Falls along the Tote Road. Between Kidney Pond and

Big Niagara Falls from Windy
Pitch Pond Trail

Daicey Pond, Nesowadnehunk Stream is relatively flat again, winding among ponds and marshy areas choked with alder. Below Daicey Pond, the stream begins a wild descent to the Penobscot River. The two largest waterfalls in this section of Nesowadnehunk Stream are Little and Big Niagara Falls.

Beginning in the mid-1800s, Nesowadnehunk Stream was the waterway used to float logs from what is now western Baxter State Park to the Penobscot River, and on to Bangor or Old Town to be milled. Nesowadnehunk Field was created as a farm to raise grain and food for the animals used in the logging operations as well as the loggers themselves. Along the Tote Road between Kidney Pond and Ledge Falls, there's a memorial cross to the unknown river driver—a testament to the dangers and wildness of Nesowadnehunk Stream.

The hike that follows the Appalachian Trail to the falls first passes the old Toll Dam, originally built in 1879. Most of the dam washed away in 1932, but part of it still clings to the far shore of the stream. This dam was used to regulate the water flow down Nesowadnehunk Stream during the log drives. It's called Toll Dam because logging companies paid toll for every log floated over the dam each spring. From the site of the Toll Dam, you can look upstream and see Mount O-J-I framed by the stream.

A short distance farther southbound on the AT, you come to a side trail to Little Niagara Falls. The trail leads out onto a flat expanse of granite that Nesowadnehunk Stream veers around before plunging into a deep pool. Rumor has it that this pool offers some of the region's best wild trout fishing. You can climb around on the rock here and get several different perspectives on Little Niagara Falls. When the stream is running low, a large sandy beach along the pool is exposed and is a good swimming spot.

Less than a mile downstream is Big Niagara Falls. The falls are somewhat higher and more of a plunge than Little Niagara Falls. The falls drops into a deep pool that collects behind a line of boulders. The stream rushes between the rocks and on down its bouldery course.

You can lengthen the hike as much as you want by following the AT as it continues along the stream past several named and unnamed falls and rapids, the last within sight of the Penobscot River. Windy Pitch is only a short walk downstream, where Nesowadnehunk Stream crashes through a jumble of huge boulders. Or you can enjoy the easy hike back to the trailhead through the evergreen forest full of rocks and moss.

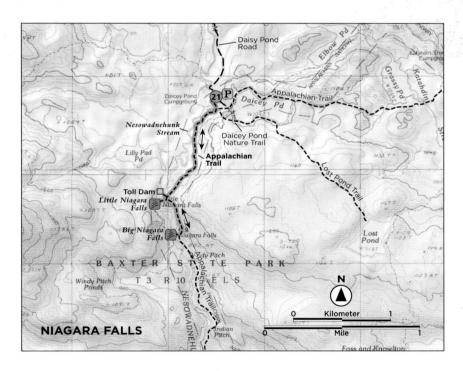

Little Niagara Falls from
Windy Pitch Pond Trail

MILES AND DIRECTIONS

0.0 Start from the southbound Appalachian Trail at the south end of the parking area.

0.1 Junction with the Daicey Pond Trail. Turn right and continue on the southbound AT.

0.8 A marked side trail leads 200 feet to the Toll Dam site on Nesowadnehunk Stream.

0.9 A marked side trail leads 300 feet to the top of Little Niagara Falls.

1.4 A marked side trail leads 500 feet to the top of Big Niagara Falls.

1.5 Arrive at the top of Big Niagara Falls. To complete the hike, return the way you came.

3.0 Arrive back at the trailhead.

22. DAICEY POND LOOP

WHY GO?

The Daicey Pond Nature Trail loops around the pond, staying close to the shore. The hike offers fine views of the surrounding mountains and a chance to find solitude without doing a lot of work. The woods are in turn cool and mossy, then angular and rocky.

THE RUN DOWN

Start: From the southbound Appalachian Trail at the south end of the day-use parking area.

Elevation gain: 140 feet.

Distance: 1.5 miles loop.

Hiking time: 1–2 hours.

Difficulty: Easy.

Seasons: May–Oct are best.

Trail surface: Woodland path.

Nearest town: Millinocket.

Other users: None.

Water availability: Daicey Pond.

Other maps: *DeLorme's The Maine Atlas and Gazetteer* map 50.

Nat Geo TOPO! Map (USGS): Doubletop Mountain.

Nat Geo Trails Illustrated Map: Baxter State Park.

FINDING THE TRAILHEAD

 From the Togue Pond Gate, drive 10.1 miles on the Park Tote Road. Turn left onto the Daicey Pond Road. Drive 1.4 miles to the day-use parking area. The trailhead is on the right at the far end of the parking area.
Trailhead GPS: N45° 52.944' / W69° 01.906'.

WHAT TO SEE

The west end of Daicey Pond can be a busy place. The area is used by thru-hikers on the Appalachian Trail, day hikers, and campers at Daicey Pond camps' cabins. Either before or after your hike, be sure to visit the camps. The view of Katahdin from the dock behind the library is one of the best in the park. Next to the library, along the shore of the pond, are two ancient white pines—maybe the oldest in the park. Daicey Pond camps were originally built in 1899 by Maurice York and named Twin Pine Camps after the still-living trees. Twin Pine Camps stayed in the York family until 1969 when the state took control.

The Daicey Pond Nature Trail leaves the AT 0.1 mile west of the camps and wanders south and east to the south shore of Daicey Pond. The trail stays close to the shore with fine views of the mountains from Doubletop Mountain to the northwest to Katahdin in the northeast.

Katahdin from Daicey Pond dock

The woods are quiet, even on weekends in the summer, cool and mossy on hot days. Take your time and count the different kinds of moss. Stop and check out their various textures. Watch for loons and ducks on the pond. Far across the pond, wisps of smoke curl up from the cabins. The occasional voice carries wordless across the water. Somehow, these distant reminders of humanity only deepen the solitude of the hike.

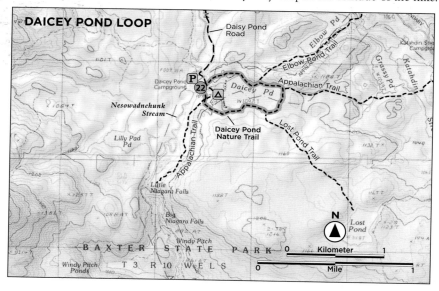

The trail hugs the east shore of Daicey Pond, passing Lost Pond Trail, then Grassy Pond Trail, before following the north shore back to the trailhead.

The north shore is rockier, more rugged. The forest looks less friendly. Past Tracy and Elbow Ponds Trail, you climb a rocky knoll and leave the pond behind.

Bright, an open forest on the north shore of Daicey Pond

MILES AND DIRECTIONS

- **0.0** Start on the southbound Appalachian Trail (AT) at the southwest end of the day-use parking area.
- **0.1** At a four-way intersection, go straight onto the Daicey Pond Nature Trail.
- **0.7** The trail loops around the Daicey Pond cabins, then follows the south shore of the pond. Pass the Lost Pond Trail.
- **0.9** The Daicey Pond Nature Trail ends at the Appalachian Trail (AT). Turn left onto the southbound AT.
- **1.1** The trail follows the north shore of Daicey Pond. Pass the Tracy and Elbow Ponds Trail.
- **1.5** The trail climbs away from Daicey Pond to arrive back at the trailhead.

23. FOSS & KNOWLTON POND

WHY GO?

Foss & Knowlton Pond is one of the prettier ponds in this corner of Baxter. You hike through a mossy forest to Lost Pond, then a dry, scrubby forest to Foss & Knowlton Pond. The view of Katahdin across the pond is worth the hike. There are lots of blueberries along the hike's second half. Both ponds have rental canoes.

THE RUN DOWN

Start: From the trailhead at the southwest end of the day-use parking area.

Elevation gain: 774 feet.

Distance: 6.8 miles out and back.

Hiking time: About 4 hours.

Difficulty: Moderate, because of the distance.

Seasons: May–Oct are best.

Trail surface: Woodland path.

Nearest town: Millinocket.

Other users: None.

Water availability: None.

Other maps: *DeLorme's The Maine Atlas and Gazetteer* map 50.

Nat Geo TOPO! Map (USGS): Doubletop Mountain, Rainbow Lake East, and Abol Pond.

Nat Geo Trails Illustrated Map: Baxter State Park.

FINDING THE TRAILHEAD

From the Togue Pond Gate, drive 10.1 miles on the Park Tote Road. Turn left onto the Daicey Pond Road. Drive 1.4 miles to the day-use parking area. The trailhead is on the right at the far end of the parking area.
Trailhead GPS: N45° 52.944' / W69° 01.906'.

WHAT TO SEE

Foss & Knowlton Pond is the farthest east and south of the ponds in the southwest corner of Baxter. To get there, you follow the Daicey Pond Nature Trail along the south shore of Daicey Pond, then the Lost Pond Trail. Lost Pond Trail crosses a rolling woodland. Like so many of the trails in this corner of the park, it passes through an evergreen forest coated with moss. The boulders, the ground, and tree trucks, everything has a luxurious coat of thick emerald. Especially in the spring or after a rain, the forest seems to glow.

The Lost Pond Trail ends along the north shore of Lost Pond, a smallish round pond tucked into the dense forest. There's a rental canoe at the trail's end if you want to explore the pond.

North shore of Foss & Knowlton Pond

The hike follows Foss & Knowlton Pond Trail east around Lost Pond. After passing the pond, the hike crosses dry, scrubby country. The ground is sandy with blueberries along the trail. The cool, mossy forest seems a distant memory.

Where the trail begins to descend to Foss & Knowlton Pond, a side trail leads to the north shore of the pond where the rental canoe is. The Foss & Knowlton Trail descends a rocky slope to the marshy shore of the pond. Large boulders sit in the water among yellow water lilies. Dragonflies clatter through the air in pursuit of prey. A bench sits beside the trail where you have a fine view of Katahdin. The trail continues along the southwest shore of the pond to the outlet, where several private canoes are parked. You can hear, but not see, the outlet stream tumbling out of the pond. The view of Katahdin across the bouldery pond is quite nice. Take a few moments to enjoy the view and munch on some blueberries.

The Foss & Knowlton Trail continues another 2.3 miles to the AT (0.5 mile from Abol Bridge), but the hike returns to the trailhead from this point.

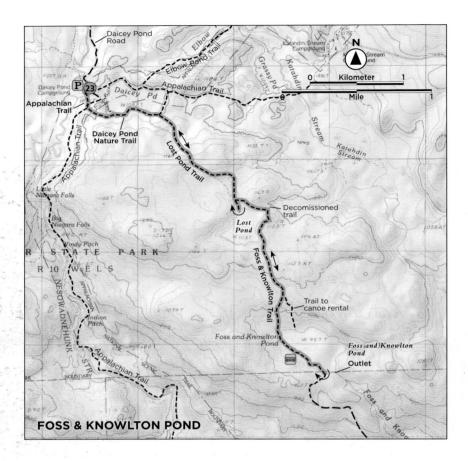

FOSS & KNOWLTON POND

MILES AND DIRECTIONS

0.0 Start on the southbound Appalachian Trail (AT) at the southwest end of the day-use parking area.

0.1 At a four-way intersection, go straight onto the Daicey Pond Nature Trail.

0.7 The trail loops around the Daicey Pond cabins, then follows the south shore of the pond. Turn right onto Lost Pond Trail.

1.6 Pass the Foss & Knowlton Trail.

1.7 Descend to the north shore of Lost Pond. To continue the hike, return to the junction with the Foss & Knowlton Trail.

1.8 Turn right onto the Foss & Knowlton Trail.

2.1 Bear right, passing a decommissioned trail.

2.3 Take a short side trail to the shore of Lost Pond.

Katahdin from near Foss & Knowlton's outlet

2.7   Pass the side trail that leads to the rental canoe on the north shore of Foss & Knowlton Pond.

3.2   The trail descends to the shore of Foss & Knowlton Pond, where there's a bench with a fine view of Katahdin.

3.5   Arrive at the outlet at the bottom of Foss & Knowlton Pond. To complete the hike, return the way you came.

6.8   Arrive back at the trailhead.

24. **GRASSY POND LOOP**

WHY GO?

This hike passes four ponds: Tracy, Elbow, Daicey, and Grassy. It's a really good hike to take in the morning or evening to see wildlife. The ponds are generally shallow and filled with aquatic plants. From several places along the hike, you have fine views of the mountains north and west. Grassy and Elbow Ponds have rental canoes.

THE RUN DOWN

Start: From the Grassy Pond Trailhead on the south side of the Park Tote Road, 200 feet west of the trailhead parking area.

Elevation gain: 482 feet.

Distance: 3.6 miles lollipop.

Hiking time: 2–3 hours.

Difficulty: Easy.

Seasons: May–Oct are best.

Trail surface: Woodland path.

Nearest town: Millinocket.

Other users: None.

Water availability: None.

Other maps: *DeLorme's The Maine Atlas and Gazetteer* map 50.

Nat Geo TOPO! Map (USGS): Doubletop Mountain.

Nat Geo Trails Illustrated Map: Baxter State Park.

FINDING THE TRAILHEAD

From the Togue Pond Gate, drive 8.5 miles on the Park Tote Road. The Grassy Pond Trailhead parking is on the left. The trailhead is 200 feet farther west on the south side of the road.
Trailhead GPS: N45° 53.458' / W69° 00.598'.

WHAT TO SEE

Tracy, Elbow, and Grassy Ponds are all fairly shallow ponds with lots of aquatic plants growing in them. Great places to find moose and other wildlife.

Tracy Pond is the first and smallest pond. Sedges and other plants grow out from the shore almost to its center. A few rocks rest among the greenery in the shallow water. Doubletop Mountain rests atop the dense forest across the pond. Watch for moose and ducks.

The trail crosses Tracy Pond's outlet stream on a rough bridge. The marshy stream is a good place to see deer, moose, and beaver. Land, pond, forest, and marsh, all blend together into one green lushness.

Katahdin across Grassy Pond on a stormy evening

A short hike through drier woods leads to Elbow Pond. Across the open water is the elbow. The pond reaches around a densely wooded point. To its right, the water is mostly open with a sedged fringe; to the left, the pond is overgrown and meadowy. The trail follows along this arm of the pond. There are places where you can venture out of the woods toward the marshy pond. Don't be too distracted by the fine view of Mount O-J-I to watch for ducks and moose.

Past Elbow Pond, the trail crosses higher ground to Daicey Pond. You turn left onto the AT and follow it to the Grassy Pond Trail at the east end of Daicey Pond. The trail crosses through a mixed forest to Grassy Pond. The best view is down the short side trail where the rental canoe is kept. Looking north across Grassy Pond, you can see the line of mountains from Mount O-J-I to Katahdin. The shore of the pond is marshy, blending gradually into the woods. On the far shore, the grassy area is widest, giving the pond its name.

Bridge across Elbow Pond's outlet

The AT continues east across the swampy outlet stream to the Park Tote Road, 0.7 mile east of the trailhead. The hike backtracks west to Grassy Pond Trail. You follow this trail north along the shore of the pond. Where the stream from Elbow Pond flows in, an unmarked trail leads out to the shore of the pond. Buried under the tall grass are old bog boards you can follow to the shore of the pond. You have a fine view of the mountains here as well as the grassy north end of the pond. Watch for moose and ducks.

The trail leaves Grassy Pond and climbs a rocky knoll. Over the abundant boulders and between the rough trunks of the spruce, you get glimpses of Katahdin. You can hear the Elbow Pond outlet stream, but not see it. A quick descent brings you back to Tracy and Elbow Ponds Trail, 0.5 mile from the trailhead.

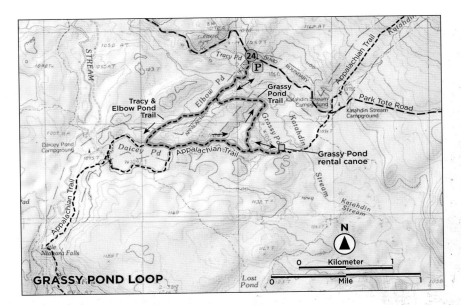

GRASSY POND LOOP

MILES AND DIRECTIONS

0.0 Start from the Grassy Pond Trailhead 200 feet west of the parking area on the Park Tote Road. In 200 feet, a side trail leads to Tracy Pond.

0.2 The Tracy and Elbow Ponds Trail goes around the east end of Tracy Pond, then crosses its outlet stream.

0.3 Arrive at Elbow Pond.

0.5 As you hike along the east shore of Elbow Pond, pass the Grassy Pond Trail.

1.1 The Tracy and Elbow Ponds Trail ends along the shore of Daicey Pond. Turn left onto the Appalachian Trail (AT).

1.3 At the east end of Daicey Pond, bear left and pass the Daicey Pond Nature Trail.

1.9 Pass the Grassy Pond Trail.

2.1 Turn left onto a side trail that leads to Grassy Pond where the rental canoe is kept. To continue the hike from the pond, return to the AT.

2.2 Turn right onto the AT.

2.4 Arrive back at the junction with the Grassy Pond Trail. Turn right onto the Grassy Pond Trail.

2.8 The trail follows the west shore of the pond to the inlet stream.

3.1 The trail climbs away from the inlet stream and ends at the Tracy and Elbow Ponds Trail. Turn right and retrace your steps to the trailhead.

3.6 Arrive back at the trailhead.

25. THE OWL

WHY GO?

The Owl is a granite dome separated from Katahdin by Witherle Ravine. The first part of the hike climbs gently through towering trees. The last mile is very steep with some exposure. The 360-degree view from the summit is spectacular. Katahdin Stream Falls, the highest in Maine, is a short walk from the junction of The Owl Trail and the Hunt Trail.

THE RUN DOWN

Start: From the Hunt Trail north of the day-use parking area in Katahdin Stream campground.

Elevation gain: 2,789 feet.

Distance: 7.0 miles out and back.

Hiking time: 6–7 hours.

Difficulty: Most strenuous, steep with exposed sections near the summit.

Seasons: June–Sept are best.

Trail surface: Woodland path and granite bedrock.

Nearest town: Millinocket.

Other users: None.

Water availability: Katahdin Stream in campground and a small stream at mile 1.5.

Other maps: *DeLorme's The Maine Atlas and Gazetteer* map 50.

Nat Geo TOPO! Map (USGS): Mount Katahdin.

Nat Geo Trails Illustrated Map: Baxter State Park.

FINDING THE TRAILHEAD

 From the Togue Pond Gate, drive 7.9 miles on the Park Tote Road. The day-use parking area is on the right in Katahdin Stream campground. The trailhead is at the back of the campground.

Trailhead GPS: N45° 53.247' / W68° 59.977'.

WHAT TO SEE

The Owl Trail climbs away from Hunt Trail a mile from the trailhead. At the junction, the tall evergreens stand straight, surrounded by lightly mossed boulders. Katahdin Stream tumbles loudly past and invisible beneath its high banks.

The trail climbs in fits and starts to a relatively level shelf. You cross a small stream, then a huge, climbable boulder. The boulder is visible from The Owl's summit, giving you a fair idea of where you hiked.

Past the boulder, the trail steepens, beginning to climb in earnest. You pass semi-open areas with views toward Katahdin. Just after a ledge with a clear view, the trail

The Owl's summit

winds through a mossy rock garden. All along this section, be on the lookout for trillium, lady slippers, and other wildflowers.

The trail becomes rockier and steeper the higher you climb. The trail tops out at the base of a high, sheer cliff. The Gateway and Witherle Ravine are just across Katahdin Stream's deep valley. Above you, The Owl appears to be an unclimbable mass of gray granite furred with bushy trees.

The trail skirts the base of the cliff and climbs very steeply through twisted and stunted trees. Way up ahead, you can see a boulder balanced atop the slope. The trail passes right next to this balanced rock to another flat at the base of a cliff. From here, you have a fine view of The Owl's summit, a short distance away.

From the summit, you have a spectacular view of Katahdin, including the Northwest Plateau and Basin. Even on clear days, misty clouds often swirl around Katahdin. To the west beyond Barren Mountain, Mounts O-J-I and Coe, and The Brothers line up across The Klondike. The scale of the granite peaks around you, and beneath your feet, is hard to comprehend. At times, voices carry across the gulf from Katahdin, a seemingly impossible distance.

On your hike back to the trailhead, take time to visit Katahdin Stream Falls. This is one of the highest waterfalls in Maine. If you count its several drops as one waterfall, it's the highest, beating out Angel Falls in western Maine. The Hunt Trail crosses the stream just below the waterfall, then climbs beside it. There's a marked side trail to an overlook with a fine view of the falls.

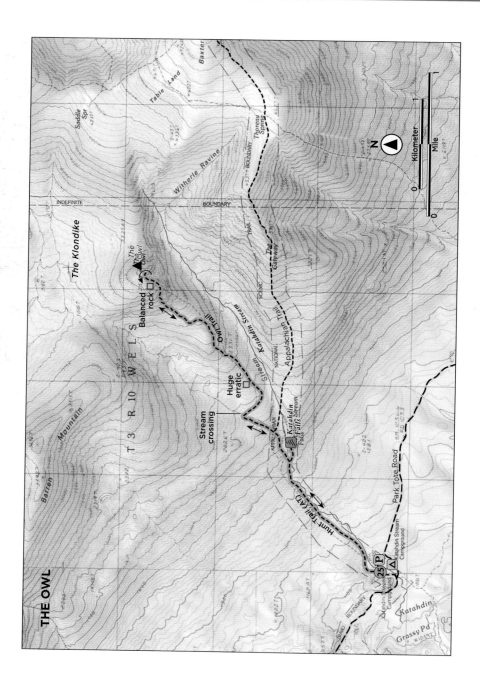

THE OWL

Descending from the summit

MILES AND DIRECTIONS

0.0 Start from the north end of the day-use parking area, following the white-blazed Hunt Trail.

1.0 Turn left onto The Owl Trail.

1.5 Cross a small stream. This is the only water source on the hike other than Katahdin Stream in the campground and below the falls.

1.9 Pass a huge erratic boulder.

2.3 First overlook.

2.9 The trail tops out to the edge of huge cliffs.

3.1 Climb very steeply to the balanced rock.

3.3 Top out to more cliffs with view of The Owl's summit.

3.5 Reach the summit. To complete the hike, return to the Hunt Trail.

6.0 Arrive back at the Hunt Trail. Turn right to return to the trailhead. **OPTION:** Turn left and follow the Hunt Trail 0.1 mile to Katahdin Stream Falls.

7.0 Arrive back at the trailhead.

26. KATAHDIN VIA THE HUNT TRAIL

WHY GO?

The Hunt Trail is the easiest and most straightforward way to climb Katahdin. The trail passes Katahdin Stream Falls, then climbs steeply, following Hunt Spur to The Gateway. There are several huge boulders to climb with the aid of iron rungs. From The Gateway, the trail crosses the flat Table Land, then climbs the summit cone to Baxter Peak with spectacular views the whole way.

THE RUN DOWN

Start: From the Hunt Trailhead at the back of the Katahdin Stream campground.

Elevation gain: 4,284 feet.

Distance: 10.0 miles out and back.

Hiking time: 7–8 hours.

Difficulty: Most strenuous.

Seasons: July–Sept are best.

Trail surface: Woodland path and exposed mountain.

Nearest town: Millinocket.

Other users: None.

Water availability: None.

Fees and permits: You need to make a reservation for a parking spot at the trailhead to ensure access. Reservations can be made online or by phone up to four months ahead.

Other maps: *DeLorme's The Maine Atlas and Gazetteer* map 50.

Nat Geo TOPO! Map (USGS): Mount Katahdin.

Nat Geo Trails Illustrated Map: Baxter State Park.

FINDING THE TRAILHEAD

From the Togue Pond Gate, drive 7.9 miles on the Park Tote Road. The day-use parking area is on the right in Katahdin Stream campground. The trailhead is at the back of the campground.
Trailhead GPS: N45° 53.247' / W68° 59.977'.

WHAT TO SEE

The Hunt Trail is the most straightforward way to climb Katahdin. It's the route the Appalachian Trail follows. Most summer days, you'll share the trail with weather-worn thru-hikers completing their 2,200-mile journey from Springer Mountain in northern Georgia. Don't feel bad if they pass you like you are standing still. Even though this is the largest climb on the entire AT, they're ready for it in ways the average hiker can't be.

Looking up Hunt Spur to
The Gateway

Baxter Peak across The Table Land
from The Gateway

The first mile, to Katahdin Stream Falls, climbs only a little. Past the falls, the climbing begins. The trail follows the spine of a ridge with fine views, mostly west and south. Less than 2.0 miles above Katahdin Stream Falls, the forest falls away and the views open up. The trees that survive this high are more like ground cover beaten down by wind and weather. It's hard not to stand and gawk at the vistas.

The trail climbs through boulder fields where iron rungs are strategically placed to aid your climb. Hunt Spur steepens and narrows as you climb. The last section below The Gateway feels like scrambling, not hiking.

At The Gateway, the trail levels out and crosses the Table Land. The wide alpine expanse is often befogged and whipped by wind. Across the Table Land, Baxter Peak is visible. The large sign at the end of the AT and the cairn that makes Katahdin a mile-high are both visible.

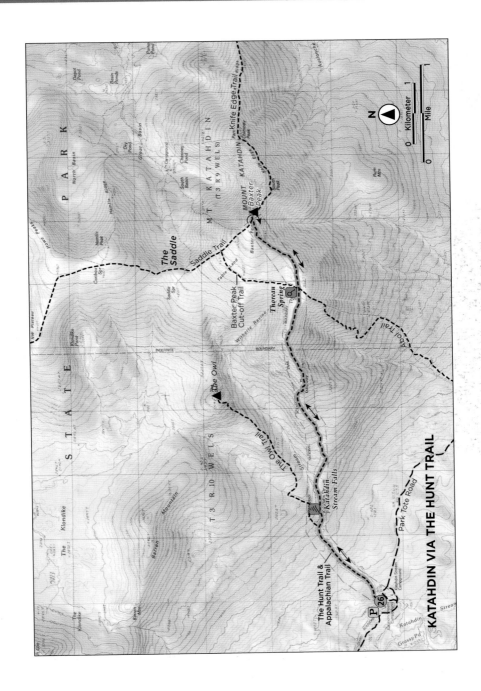

KATAHDIN VIA THE HUNT TRAIL

You pass Thoreau Spring, a usually reliable water source that does sometimes dry up—ask at the ranger station near the trailhead before relying on the spring for water. The Abol Trail joins the Hunt Trail at the spring.

The view from Baxter Peak is staggering. The mountain drops away as if scooped out. Chimney Pond rests 2,000 feet below in spruce that looks like a lawn from this height. The jagged line of the Knife Edge arcs to Pamola Peak. Everywhere you look, there are mountains, lakes, and endless forest. Ravens glide on rising thermals. They drop among the lounging hikers to cadge scraps and steal a bit of food. Thru-hikers celebrate the end of their AT and pose for pictures beside the weathered sign.

You need to make a reservation for a parking spot at the trailhead to ensure access. Reservations can be made up to four months in advance by calling (207) 723-5140 or online at http://www.baxterstateparkauthority.com.

MILES AND DIRECTIONS

0.0   Start from the Hunt Trailhead at the back of the Katahdin Stream campground.

1.1   Pass the Owl Trail.

1.2   The Hunt Trail crosses Katahdin Stream at the base of Katahdin Stream Falls and climbs to the top of the falls. This is the beginning of the real climb.

2.8   The trail steeply climbs to tree line with increasing views.

3.5   The trail climbs through a boulder field and up Hunt Spur to The Gateway.

4.2   Cross the relatively flat Table Land to Thoreau Spring. Pass Abol Trail.

5.0   Climb steadily to Baxter Peak. To complete the hike, return the way you came.

10.0   Arrive back at the trailhead.

27. **KATAHDIN VIA THE ABOL TRAIL**

WHY GO?

The Abol Trail is the shortest route to Baxter Peak on Katahdin. As you would expect, it's extremely steep. The hike offers spectacular views of the surrounding country. This hike also includes a hike around the base of Baxter Peak through the Table Land. In 2016, Abol Trail was rerouted away from a dangerous slide. The new trail offers more expansive views than the old trail.

THE RUN DOWN

Start: From the ranger's station at the Abol campground, across the Park Tote Road from the day-use parking.

Elevation gain: 4,051 feet.

Distance: 8.4 miles lollipop.

Hiking time: 6–8 hours.

Difficulty: Most strenuous.

Seasons: July–Sept are best.

Trail surface: Woodland path and exposed bedrock.

Nearest town: Millinocket.

Other users: None.

Water availability: Abol Stream in the campground.

Fees and permits: You need to make a reservation for a parking spot at the trailhead to ensure access. Reservations can be made online or by phone up to four months ahead.

Other maps: *DeLorme's The Maine Atlas and Gazetteer* map 50.

Nat Geo TOPO! Map (USGS): Mount Katahdin and Abol Pond.

Nat Geo Trails Illustrated Map: Baxter State Park.

FINDING THE TRAILHEAD

 From the Togue Pond Gate, drive 5.6 miles on the Park Tote Road. The day-use parking area is across the road from Abol campground. The hike starts at the ranger's station.

Trailhead GPS: N45° 52.418' / W68° 57.838'.

WHAT TO SEE

On September 6, 1846, Henry David Thoreau and his party camped at the mouth of Abol Stream—where today there's a commercial campground. It'd taken Thoreau a week to get here from Bangor by canoe and foot.

The next day, the group bushwhacked toward Katahdin. They forced their way through the forest and up the stream. They stopped for the night at about 3,800 feet

Hikers on the steep rocks
below Abol Gateway

Approaching Baxter Peak

on the shoulder of the mountain. Thoreau continued up in fading light. He forced his way through the upper reaches of Abol Stream, soaking himself. Finally, he left the stream and climbed directly toward the Table Land. At one point, Thoreau was forced to clamber atop Krumholtz spruce before reaching bare rock. He never made it to the summit, turned back by darkness and then the next day by a gale.

There's been much debate as to Thoreau's exact route up Katahdin. No one knows for sure, but it was near today's Abol Trail—probably just to its east. Needless to say, a hike up the Abol Trail is much easier than the route Thoreau followed. Still, it's the shortest and steepest trail up Katahdin.

The first mile climbs gently, then steadily through a hardwood forest to the gravelly outflow of a large slide that occurred in 1816. From this area, you have several views of the climb ahead. The trail used to ascend the slide, but several years ago it became dangerously unstable. A new trail slabs west, switchbacking up a ridge. On the steep ridge, you break out of the trees. To your west is Hunt Spur, which the AT follows, and behind you the expanse of the North Woods. Ahead is the naked granite flank of Katahdin. Notice the weather-shaped boulders along the trail.

The trail slabs back east and rejoins the original trail at the top of the slide. From here, it's a short, extremely steep climb to the Table Land. A large cairn welcomes you to Katahdin's cloud factory. The trail continues to Thoreau Spring, ending at the Hunt Trail; Thoreau never made it this far.

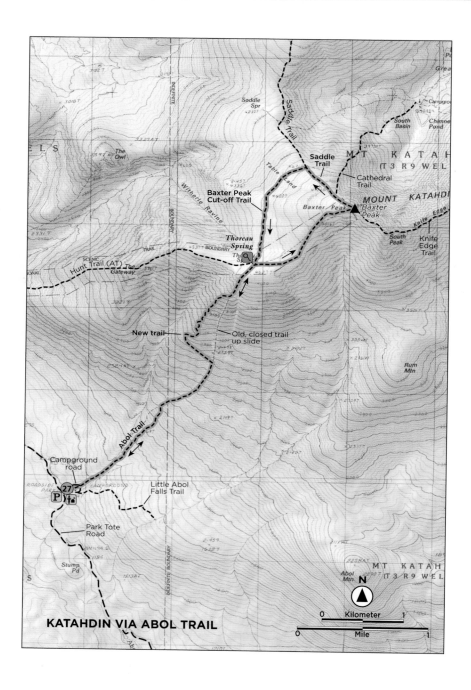

KATAHDIN VIA ABOL TRAIL

A steady climb brings you to Baxter Peak. After taking in the view from Maine's highest point, descend northwest on the Saddle Trail. About halfway down to The Saddle, turn left onto Baxter Peak Cut-off. This trail slabs around the summit to Thoreau Spring. Along the way, you have fine views of the Northwest Plateau, Witherle Ravine, and The Owl. The trail wanders through a rock garden carpeted with rich green shrubs and stunted trees.

Back at Thoreau Spring, you retrace your steps down Abol Trail. Remember, descending is more dangerous than climbing, especially after a hard day of hiking.

You need to make a reservation for a parking spot at the trailhead to ensure access. Reservations can be made up to four months in advance by calling (207) 723-5140 or online at http://www.baxterstateparkauthority.com.

MILES AND DIRECTIONS

0.0 Start from the ranger's station at Abol campground, across the Park Tote Road from the day-use parking area.

0.1 Walk through the campground. Abol Trail begins between lean-tos 11 and 12.

1.5 The trail climbs gently, then steadily. Bear left off the rocky trail onto the new section of trail.

2.5 The trail switchbacks steeply up. Break out of the trees for good with fine views.

2.6 The new trail ends atop the slide.

2.8 The trail climbs extremely steep to the Table Land.

3.0 Reach Thoreau Spring. Turn right onto Hunt Trail.

4.0 Climb steadily to Baxter Peak. Turn left and descend on the Saddle Trail. **OPTION:** You can simply return from Baxter Peak the way you came for an 8.0-mile out and back hike.

4.5 Descend steeply, passing Cathedral Trail. Turn left onto Baxter Peak Cut-off Trail.

5.1 Pass the head of Witherle Ravine.

5.4 Arrive back at Thoreau Spring. Cross Hunt Trail onto Abol Trail.

8.4 Arrive back at the trailhead.

28. LITTLE ABOL FALLS

WHY GO?

Little Abol Falls is an easy walk from Abol campground. The trail climbs very little along its route through a hardwood forest. The falls are on one of the branches of Abol Stream. Above the falls, the stream tumbles through mossy boulders over smooth, orange granite. The falls drop 15 feet into a shallow pool of similar granite littered with rounded stones. It's a picturesque falls and a good place to cool off on a hot day.

THE RUN DOWN

Start: From the ranger's station at Abol campground, across the Park Tote Road from the day-use parking area.

Elevation gain: 341 feet.

Distance: 1.8 miles out and back.

Hiking time: About 1 hour.

Difficulty: Easy.

Seasons: May–Oct are best.

Trail surface: Woodland path.

Nearest town: Millinocket.

Other users: None.

Water availability: None.

Other maps: *DeLorme's The Maine Atlas and Gazetteer* map 50.

Nat Geo TOPO! Map (USGS): Abol Pond.

Nat Geo Trails Illustrated Map: Baxter State Park.

FINDING THE TRAILHEAD

 From the Togue Pond Gate, drive 5.6 miles on the Park Tote Road. The day-use parking area is across the road from Abol campground. The hike starts at the ranger's station.

Trailhead GPS: N45° 52.417' / W68° 57.837.

WHAT TO SEE

The several branches of Abol Stream drain the south face of Katahdin. The stream's name is shortened from the Penobscot word "Abalajakomejus," which roughly translates as treeless expanse—probably a reference to the slide Abol Trail originally followed. The slide is high on the face of Katahdin between the branches of the stream.

The branches of the stream come together in a marshy area south and east of Stump Pond. The stream then flows south toward the west end of Abol Pond. The stream turns west, joined by Abol Pond's outflow. It meanders through marshy lowlands from there to the West Branch at Abol Bridge.

Little Abol Falls

HIKING WITH YOUNG CHILDREN

For children, hiking is more about the process than the destination. Take time to explore as you hike. Check out the toads, climb on boulders, throw rocks into ponds and waterfalls, and collect pine cones. If you make the process fun and adventurous, you'll be shocked by how far kids can go and how easily they'll handle challenging hikes. Even children as young as four can climb a mountain if properly motivated. And with kids along, the adults will see and find things they'd otherwise miss.

Bring plenty of high energy snacks like fruit or even candy and make sure everyone drinks enough water. Kids need to refuel more frequently than adults. The adults sometimes don't realize the kids need food or water until they get grumpy.

Remember the return hike is always harder. Everyone is tired and more prone to stumbling. Try making a game out of it. Turn the return hike into a moving game of hide-and-seek, have a contest to find more different colored mushrooms than anyone else, or be the first one to touch every tree with a blaze on it.

Little Abol Falls is on the east branch of Abol Stream. There's no Big Abol Falls, but there's an Abol Falls on the West Branch just downstream from Abol Bridge.

The hike to the falls follows an old woods road through a hardwood forest. You climb gradually—250 feet over the hike. The trail ends at the top of the falls. The stream tumbles down through the woods, dropping down small granite ledges. Rounded, mossy boulders line the stream. The water rushes across smooth orange granite that shines through the shallow stream.

The stream pinches between rounded boulders and drops about 15 feet into a pool. Like above the falls, the floor of the pool is smooth granite covered with rounded cobbles. On the far side of the stream, jagged layers of bedrock poke out of the hillside. It's a fine place to cool off on a hot summer day.

Little Abol Stream below the falls rushing over red granite

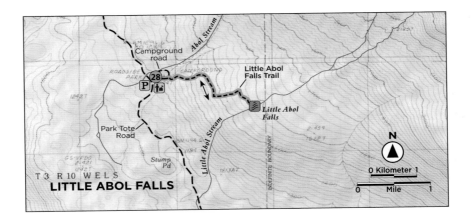

MILES AND DIRECTIONS

0.0 Start at the ranger's station at Abol campground, across the Park Tote Road from the day-use parking area.

0.1 Walk through the campground, staying to the right. The marked trailhead is between sites 8 and 10. In 100 feet, the wide trail fords a rushing stream.

0.9 The trail climbs gently to Little Abol Falls. To complete the hike, return the way you came.

1.8 Arrive back at the trailhead.

29. BLUEBERRY LEDGES

WHY GO?
Blueberry Ledges is a huge expanse of semi-open granite bedrock that Katahdin Stream slides down. On and around the ledges grow birch trees and, of course, blueberries. It's one of the most extraordinary sights in Baxter. The hike reaches the ledges from the south, beginning at Abol Beach. This route follows Abol Stream with fine views of Katahdin, before turning north toward Blueberry Ledges.

THE RUN DOWN
Start: From the Abol Stream Trailhead at the end of the Abol Beach Road.

Elevation gain: 740 feet.

Distance: 6.5 miles out and back off a loop

Hiking time: 3–4 hours.

Difficulty: Moderate.

Seasons: May–Oct are best.

Trail surface: Woodland path.

Land Status: Baxter State Park and Appalachian Trail corridor.

Nearest town: Millinocket. There's a store and a restaurant at Abol Bridge, 0.5 mile off the hike.

Other users: Hunting is permitted in season. The section of Abol Stream Trail outside Baxter State Park is sometimes used by ATVs.

Water availability: None.

Other maps: *DeLorme's The Maine Atlas and Gazetteer* map 50.

Nat Geo TOPO! Map (USGS): Abol Pond.

Nat Geo Trails Illustrated Map: Baxter State Park.

FINDING THE TRAILHEAD

From the Togue Pond Gate, drive 3.0 miles on the Park Tote Road. Turn left onto the Abol Beach Road. Drive 0.5 mile to the end of the road. The trailhead is at the end of the road.
Trailhead GPS: N45° 50.410' / W68° 56.347'.

WHAT TO SEE
The Blueberry Ledges Trail runs 4.4 miles from the Tote Road just east of Katahdin Stream campground to the Appalachian Trail near Abol Bridge. Along its course, the trail descends about 500 feet. The ledges are 1.4 miles north of the AT and 3.0 miles south of the Tote Road. This hike gets to Blueberry Ledges from the south, using the Abol Stream Trail that begins at Abol Beach picnic area.

Blueberry Ledges is a huge, semi-open expanse of bare granite that Katahdin Stream slides down. There are numerous slides, sluices, waterfalls, and, of course, lots

Blueberry Ledges

of blueberries growing where they can on the broken bedrock around and beneath small birch trees. It's one of the most extraordinary sights in Baxter. You could spend hours exploring the ledges and falls and not see it all.

To get there, follow the Abol Stream Trail west from Abol Beach. The trail crosses a sandy esker, then parallels Abol Stream. The stream moves languidly through low, marshy country. To the north, the land rises, forested from this wetland to Katahdin. The mountain is visible along much of the trail. The second half of this trail is outside the park and is used occasionally by ATVs and snowmobiles.

The trail ends at the AT at a spot about a half mile from Abol Bridge. Follow the AT north back into the park. From the bridge over Abol Stream, you have your last view of Katahdin. The trail loops around the deadwater at the mouth of Abol Stream. Across the swampy pool is a commercial campground on the spot where Thoreau camped in 1846.

At the large AT kiosk, bear right onto Abol Pond Trail. From here, you hike north over sandy soil through a birch forest. The trail climbs very gently.

One of several waterfalls downstream from Blueberry Ledges

A mile north of the AT, the trail crosses a granite ledge. You can hear Katahdin Stream to your left. Two unmarked, but obvious, side trails descend to the stream. Each trail visits a good-sized waterfall. This is the base of Blueberry Ledges.

The trail crosses more open granite before reaching the main area of Blueberry Ledges. The trail bears right and climbs away from the ledges, but you need to follow the open granite down to Katahdin Stream. Take time to explore the area, looking for hidden sluices and waterfalls. If you visit in late summer, snack on the abundant blueberries. But remember, where the stream slides down the bare rock can be slippery, footing can be uneven. Take care.

On the return hike, follow Abol Pond Trail. This trail crosses semi-open sandy areas and passes an extremely long beaver dam before descending to an interesting "bridge" over Abol Stream.

This hike is about the same distance as hiking directly to Blueberry Ledges from the north, but infinitely more varied and interesting.

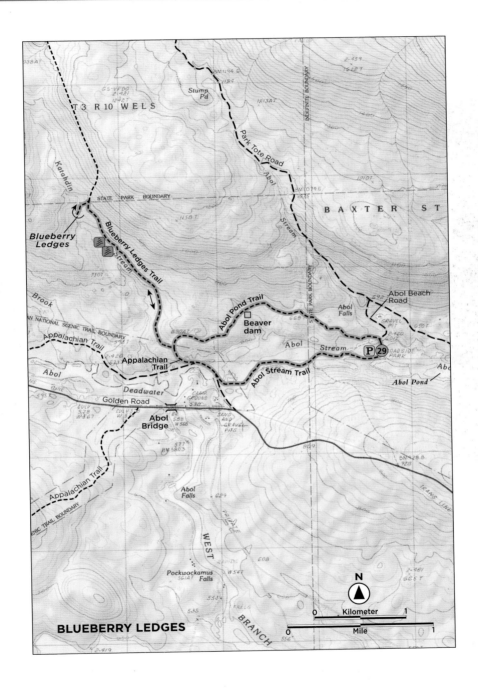

BLUEBERRY LEDGES

MILES AND DIRECTIONS

0.0 Start from the Abol Stream Trailhead at the end of Abol Beach Road.

1.2 The trail follows Abol Stream with views of Katahdin and the marshy stream. The trail ends at the Appalachian Trail. Turn right, heading northbound. **OPTION:** From this junction, it's 0.5 mile southbound on the AT to Abol Bridge where there's a store and a restaurant.

1.5 The trail crosses Abol Stream and arrives at a junction where there's a large information kiosk. Bear right onto the Abol Pond Trail.

1.7 Go straight onto the Blueberry Ledges Trail.

2.5 Where the trail crosses a granite ledge and you can hear Katahdin Stream, an unmarked side trail on the left leads 300 feet to a waterfall at the base of Blueberry Ledges. After exploring around the falls, return to the Blueberry Ledges Trail.

2.6 Just past the first side trail, turn left onto another unmarked side trail.

2.7 The side trail crosses open ledges. At a stone fire ring, turn left and descend to Katahdin Stream where there's a huge log jam. A waterfall is visible just upstream. After exploring this waterfall, return to the Blueberry Ledges Trail.

3.2 The trail emerges onto the open ledges. Turn left off the trail and follow the granite bedrock to Katahdin Stream. To complete the hike, return on Blueberry Ledges Trail the way you came.

4.8 Arrive back at the Abol Pond Trail. Turn left.

5.4 The trail passes along the base of a very long beaver dam.

6.3 The trail crosses Abol Stream.

6.4 The Abol Pond Trail ends at the Abol Beach Road. Turn right and follow the road.

6.5 Arrive back at the trailhead.

30. KETTLE POND

WHY GO?

The Kettle Pond Trail begins just north of Abol Beach. The trail skirts Abol Pond, then crosses the Tote Road. North of the Tote Road, the trail passes near several kettle ponds before ending at the Tote Road. This is a good hike for a quiet stroll to find wildflowers and mushrooms. Watch for deer and moose near the ponds and bogs.

THE RUN DOWN

Start: From the picnic area at the end of the Abol Beach Road.

Elevation gain: 264 feet.

Distance: 2.0 miles shuttle hike.

Hiking time: About 1 hour.

Difficulty: Easy.

Seasons: May–Oct are best.

Trail surface: Woodland path.

Nearest town: Millinocket.

Other users: Hunting is permitted in season.

Water availability: None.

Other maps: *DeLorme's The Maine Atlas and Gazetteer* map.

Nat Geo TOPO! Map (USGS): Abol Pond.

Nat Geo Trails Illustrated Map: Baxter State Park.

FINDING THE TRAILHEAD

From the Togue Pond Gate, drive 3.0 miles on the Park Tote Road. Turn left onto the Abol Beach Road. Drive 0.5 mile to the end of the road. The trailhead is at the end of the road.

Trailhead GPS: N45° 50.410' / W68° 56.347'.

WHAT TO SEE

Abol Pond is a long, irregularly shaped lake bounded by a large esker on the north. The Tote Road crosses the esker from the South Gate to Abol Beach Road. North of the esker are numerous small kettle ponds. Kettle ponds form when retreating glaciers break apart. Large chunks of ice depress the ground. When the ice melts, a kettle pond is left behind. Many of these ponds—such as Cranberry Pond—shrink over time, eventually becoming bogs or meadows. The Kettle Pond Trail passes several such ponds in various states of evolution.

The trailhead is east from Abol Beach Road along the north shore of Abol Pond. This section of trail was a woods road in the past. The trail climbs away from the pond through a stand of towering pines. You're hiking over the esker.

One of the small kettle ponds
along the trail

Across the Tote Road, the trail drops down off the esker. You pass several large boulders sitting in the woods. Notice that down off the esker, the forest is wetter and the trees mostly hardwoods. The elevation here is barely 600 feet above sea level.

The trail passes several small ponds, some no larger than vernal pools. Take your time and watch for moose feeding in the water or using the trail. The largest pond you pass, visible through the trees on the right, is Kettle Pond. Abol and Kettle Ponds are separated by the narrowest neck of eroded esker that the Tote Road crosses.

The trail crosses a good-sized stream on a new bridge. This stream drains much of Abol Mountain that rises to 2,292 feet to the north. Past the bridge, the trail follows the base of the esker. You pass several more tiny ponds before reaching the end of the trail and the Tote Road.

A side trail leads 0.1 mile farther east to Caverly Pond. From its south shore where there's a rental canoe, you have a spectacular view of Katahdin. The mountain's summit is less than 5.0 miles away, but more than 4,500 feet higher.

Along Kettle Pond Trail on a rainy summer day

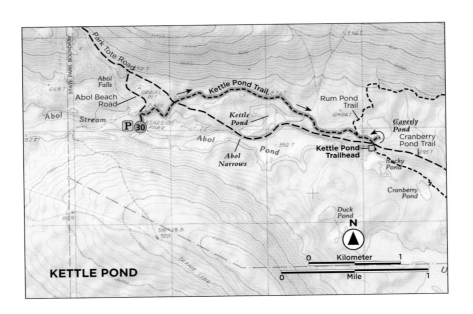

KETTLE POND

MILES AND DIRECTIONS

0.0 Start from the picnic area at the end of the Abol Beach Road. Follow the road north from the beach.

0.1 Turn right onto Kettle Pond Trail.

0.5 The trail follows the north shore of Abol Pond, then turns north and climbs gently through pines to the Tote Road.

0.6 Cross the Tote Road and descend into a mixed forest. Pass several huge boulders and small unnamed ponds.

1.2 Pass just north of Kettle Pond.

1.4 Cross a stream on a bridge.

1.9 The trail skirts the base of the esker crossed by the Tote Road. Pass Rum Pond Trail.

2.0 The trail passes another small pond. Reach the trail's end at the Tote Road. A side trail leads 0.1 mile to Caverly Pond.

31. CRANBERRY POND

WHY GO?

Cranberry Pond is a beautiful little pond ringed by a dense mat of sphagnum moss and cranberries. Bog plants such as pitcher plants are common. The trail to the pond passes through a hardwood forest with a varied understory. You pass Rocky Pond near the trailhead. The hike can be extended to include Togue Pond, some interesting wetlands, and a stand of mature red pines.

THE RUN DOWN

Start: From the Cranberry Pond Trailhead on the south side of the Park Tote Road, across from the Kettle Pond Trailhead parking.

Elevation gain: 172 feet.

Distance: 1.2 miles out and back.

Hiking time: About 1 hour.

Difficulty: Easy.

Seasons: May–Oct are best.

Trail surface: Woodland path and bog boardwalk.

Nearest town: Millinocket.

Other users: Hunting is permitted in season.

Water availability: Rocky Pond, near the trailhead.

Other maps: *DeLorme's The Maine Atlas and Gazetteer* map 50.

Nat Geo TOPO! Map (USGS): Abol Pond.

Nat Geo Trails Illustrated Map: Baxter State Park.

FINDING THE TRAILHEAD

From the Togue Pond Gate, drive 1.2 miles on the Park Tote Road. The Kettle Pond Trailhead parking is a small turnout on the right. The Cranberry Pond Trailhead is across the road.
Trailhead GPS: N45° 50.276' / W68° 54.467'.

WHAT TO SEE

Cranberry Pond is a small, roundish pond rimmed by rafts of thick sphagnum moss and cranberries. Pitcher plants and other bog denizens are common. A short board-walk leads across marshy ground to the edge of the pond.

The hike begins across the Tote Road from the Kettle Pond Trailhead. You descend to the shore of Rocky Pond. The trail passes through a hardwood forest with varied understory. A good hike for spring wildflowers. In no time, you reach the boardwalk that heads out to Cranberry Pond. You pass through pines, then tall shrubs before reaching the mat of moss and cranberries. The pond is a small, quiet pool.

The boardwalk to Cranberry Pond

You can hike straight back to the trailhead, or continue east on Cranberry Pond Trail. It parallels the Tote Road through a stand of huge red pines. Beyond the pines, the trail skirts around some snag-filled wetlands before reaching the north shore of Upper Togue Pond out of sight of the beach. The trail turns away from the pond and continues to the Tote Road, 0.1 mile from the gatehouse and 0.3 mile from the beach on Togue Pond.

MILES AND DIRECTIONS

0.0   Start from the Cranberry Pond Trailhead on the south side of the Park Tote Road, across from the Kettle Pond Trailhead parking. The trail drops down to Rocky Pond in 350 feet.

0.5   Turn left onto the Cranberry Pond boardwalk.

0.6   The boardwalk ends on the shore of Cranberry Pond. To complete the hike, return the way you came. **OPTION:** You can continue east on Cranberry Pond Trail another 0.9 mile to the Tote Road between Togue Pond and the Togue Pond Gate. This would make a 1.6-mile shuttle hike or a 3.0-mile out and back hike.

1.2   Arrive back at the trailhead.

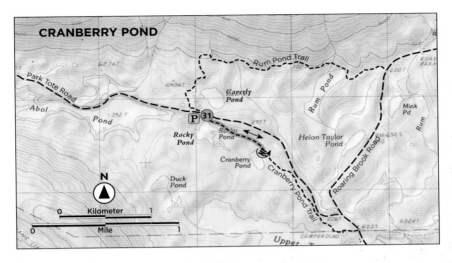

Pitcher plant in bloom on the boggy fringe of Cranberry Pond

32. RUM POND

WHY GO?

The Rum Pond Trail passes low across the shoulder of Abol Mountain through a beautiful and varied evergreen forest. The hike visits Rum and Caverly Ponds. From the south shore of Caverly Pond, you have a fine view of Katahdin.

THE RUN DOWN

Start: From the Kettle Pond Trailhead on the north side of the Park Tote Road.

Elevation gain: 250 feet.

Distance: 2.3 miles shuttle hike.

Hiking time: 1–2 hours.

Difficulty: Easy.

Seasons: May–Oct are best.

Trail surface: Woodland path.

Nearest town: Millinocket.

Other users: Hunting is permitted in season.

Water availability: Caverly Pond at mile 0.1.

Other maps: *DeLorme's The Maine Atlas and Gazetteer* map.

Nat Geo TOPO! Map (USGS): Abol Pond.

Nat Geo Trails Illustrated Map: Baxter State Park.

FINDING THE TRAILHEAD

 From the Togue Pond Gate, drive 1.2 miles on the Park Tote Road. The Kettle Pond Trailhead parking is a small turnout on the right. The trailhead is on the north side of the road.

Trailhead GPS: N45° 50.290' / W68° 54.485'.

WHAT TO SEE

The Park Tote Road crosses an esker just west of the south gate. On both sides of the esker are small scenic ponds. Many of these are kettle ponds formed by the retreating glaciers. The last remaining chunks of ice created depressions in the ground that became the ponds. The hike to begins in the middle of this glacial terrain.

From the trailhead, a short level walk on a wide trail leads to the south shore of Caverly Pond. This kettle pond used to be named Round Pond, but was renamed for long-time Baxter director Buzz Caverly, following his retirement in 2005. There's a rental canoe here. The south shore of the pond offers a spectacular view of Katahdin across the scenic pond. The trail continues around the east side of the pond to a rocky outcropping.

Rum Pond

Katahdin across
Caverly Pond

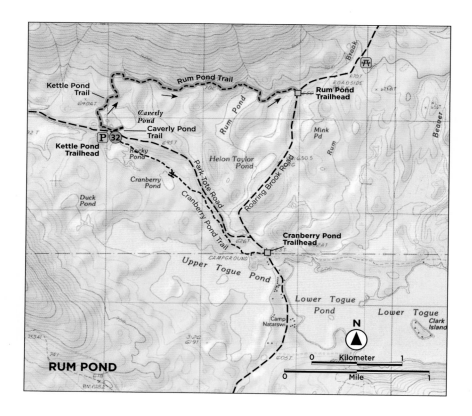

The Kettle Pond Trailhead heads west all the way to Abol Beach, passing several small kettle ponds. To reach Rum Pond, head north on Rum Pond Trail. The trail loops around the west end of Caverly Pond—seen shining through the woods—and turns west toward Rum Pond.

The trail wanders through a forest of mature trees, including stands of red pines, and large boulders. Both ends of this trail are old woods roads, but the middle section is rough and rocky. The forest is varied and interesting as you slab around the base of Abol Mountain—the highlight of the hike.

Just before reaching Rum Pond, the trail crosses a small, weeping stream. You cross on bog boards, then the trail widens to an old roadbed. Rum Pond can be seen to the south through the trees. The trail doesn't come right to the pond, but there are several places where you can easily bushwhack the 100 feet to the shore. Rum Pond is long and narrow, arching away to the south. Evergreens crowd the rocky shore. Here and there, shrubs tumble down from the trees to the water. Angular boulders stick out of the shallows. Loons rest on the surface between dives for fish.

The trail loops around to the west, then climbs gently to Roaring Brook Road. There's no parking at the trailhead, but Rum Brook picnic area is 0.2 mile north on the road.

MILES AND DIRECTIONS

0.0 Start from the Kettle Pond Trailhead on the north side of the Park Tote Road next to the parking area. Bear right from the trailhead toward Caverly Pond.

0.1 Reach the south shore of Caverly Pond. To continue the hike, return to the Kettle Pond Trail.

0.2 Turn right onto the Kettle Pond Trail.

0.4 Turn right onto Rum Pond Trail.

1.9 Reach the north end of Rum Pond.

2.3 Reach the Rum Pond Trailhead on Roaring Brook Road.

33. SOUTH TURNER MOUNTAIN

WHY GO?

The summit of South Turner Mountain offers the best view of Katahdin from the east. The hike is relatively flat, to and around Sandy Stream Pond. There are three side trails of bog boards to the pond that give you a chance to look for moose and ducks. Beyond the pond, the trail is very steep up South Turner Mountain. The final push to the summit ascends a slide of loose rocks. From the summit, you not only have a spectacular view of Katahdin, but can also see almost all of Baxter State Park and the North Woods beyond.

THE RUN DOWN

Start: From the Roaring Brook ranger's station at the north end of the parking area. Remember to sign in for the hike.

Elevation gain: 1,718 feet.

Distance: 4.0 miles out and back.

Hiking time: 3–4 hours.

Difficulty: Strenuous. The second mile of the hike climbs more than 1,500 feet.

Seasons: June–Sept are best.

Trail surface: Woodland path and rock slide to the summit.

Nearest town: Millinocket.

Other users: None.

Water availability: Roaring Brook near the trailhead, Sandy Stream at mile 0.8, and a spring at mile 1.6.

Fees and permits: A reservation to park at the trailhead is highly recommended. Reservations can be made up to three months in advance by calling 723-5140 or online at baxterstateparkauthority.com.

Other maps: *DeLorme's The Maine Atlas and Gazetteer* map 51.

Nat Geo TOPO! Map (USGS): Katahdin Lake.

Nat Geo Trails Illustrated Map: Baxter State Park.

FINDING THE TRAILHEAD

From the Togue Pond Gate at the south entrance, turn right onto the Roaring Brook Road. Drive 8.0 miles to the end of the road. Hiker parking is in the lot to the left. The hike begins at the ranger station—where you need to sign in before hiking—at the north end of the parking area.
Trailhead GPS: N45° 55.180' / W68° 51.444'.

WHAT TO SEE

Every morning throughout the summer, dozens of cars pull into the parking lot at the end of the Roaring Brook Road. Hikers get out and mill around, readying themselves. In dribbles and drabs, they head into the woods. Almost all of them are

South Turner Mountain from the boardwalk on Sandy Stream Pond

hiking up Katahdin to look out across the seemingly endless North Woods. Very few of them head to other trails to explore those endless woods or to climb other mountains and gaze at Katahdin. The hike from Roaring Brook to South Turner Mountain offers the chance to do both.

The hike begins at the often-crowded Roaring Brook ranger's station, crosses Roaring Brook, and disappears into the solitude of the woods. The trail skirts around Sandy Stream Pond where there are three short side trails of bog boards that go to the pond's edge. In the morning or evening, this is one of the best places in Baxter State Park to find moose. Often fingers of mist drift over the pond as ducks quietly bob on the water. South Turner Mountain rises steeply to the north.

The trail loops around the pond, crosses Sandy Stream, and then heads toward South Turner Mountain. The trail becomes a boulder hop for a few hundred yards,

Looking down the slide
to Sandy Stream Pond

then begins to climb. The trail climbs relentlessly through a mixed, hardwood forest. A little less than half way up the mountain, a side trail leads to a spring at the head of a small brook. The stream tumbles noisily down the mountain toward Sandy Stream. Above the spring, the trail becomes rockier and the woods transition to evergreens.

The trail arrives at a level spot at the bottom of a slide. To the west, you can see Katahdin. Baxter Peak is hidden behind Pamola Peak, but you can look directly into

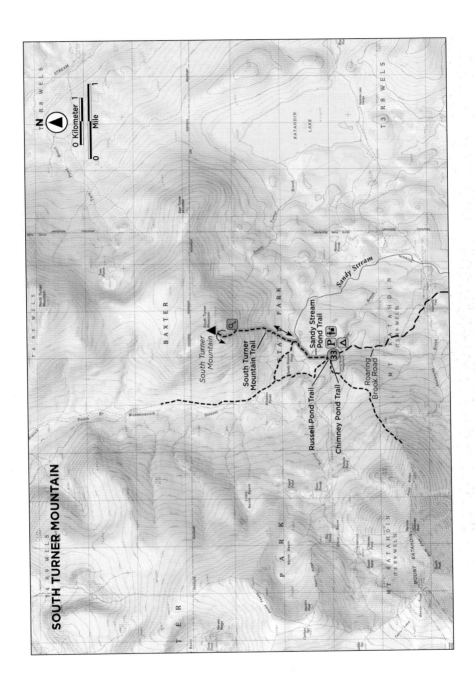

SOUTH TURNER MOUNTAIN

North Basin and see the arc of Katahdin around Great Basin. The bottom of the slide is mostly small, orangish rocks. As you look up the slide, the rocks get larger and grayer, ending at a bare bedrock dome. You can see the wooden sign on the summit, 175 feet almost straight above you. There are blazes on the rocks up the slide, but the easiest way to the summit is to pick a likely route and go. As you near the summit, the loose rock gives way to bedrock and easier climbing.

The view from the summit is unparalleled. Not only do you have the best view of Katahdin there is, but you can also see almost all of Baxter State Park. To the north, across North Turner Mountain, is The Traveler; to its west, Black Cat Mountain. Closer, you can see the mountains around Russell Pond and amazingly, Wassataquoik Lake nestled among them. Below you, to the east is Katahdin Lake and the hazy, endless woods. As you stand on the summit, turning from view to view, remember that less than 3.0 miles away nearly a hundred hikers crowd Katahdin's summits and flanks. You have South Turner Mountain all to yourself, except for maybe a scolding junco or two.

A reservation to park at the trailhead is highly recommended. Reservations can be made up to three months in advance by calling (207) 723-5140 or online at http://www.baxterstateparkauthority.com.

MILES AND DIRECTIONS

0.0 Start from the Roaring Brook ranger's station at the north end of the parking area. Be sure to sign in for the hike on the porch of the ranger's station.

400 feet Turn right onto the Russell Pond Trail and cross Roaring Brook.

0.1 Turn right onto the Sandy Stream Pond Trail.

0.5 A side trail leads to Sandy Stream Pond. This side trail loops back to the main trail.

0.6 The Big Rock Viewpoint Trail leads 100 feet to Sandy Stream Pond.

0.7 The trail crosses Sandy Stream.

0.8 A side trail leads 100 feet to Sandy Stream Pond.

0.9 Turn right onto the South Turner Mountain Trail.

1.6 The South Turner Mountain Trail is flat, winding among and over boulders for 0.1 mile, then climbs steadily to the side trail that leads 200 feet to a spring.

1.9 Past the spring, the trail steepens, coming out at the bottom of a slide.

2.1 The trail climbs the slide to the summit. The open summit has 360-degree views. To complete the hike, return the way you came.

4.0 Arrive back at the trailhead. Remember to sign out at the ranger's station.

34. **NORTH PEAKS**

WHY GO?

The hike follows Chimney Pond Trail, then climbs the incredibly steep Hamlin Ridge. The sides of which drop away almost vertically. You have spectacular views in every direction. From Hamlin Peak, you descend to Caribou Spring, then cross a series of loose-rocked summits arrayed atop North Basin's nearly vertical headwall. These summits are collectively known as the North Peaks. From the fifth peak, the trail turns north and descends across a series of knobs to tree line with fine views.

THE RUN DOWN

Start: From the Roaring Brook Trailhead at the north end of the day-use parking area.

Elevation gain: 3,621 feet.

Distance: 14.0 miles out and back.

Hiking time: 8–9 hours.

Difficulty: Most strenuous.

Seasons: June–Sept are best.

Trail surface: Very rocky woodland path and bare bedrock.

Nearest town: Millinocket.

Other users: None.

Water availability: Roaring Brook near the trailhead and Caribou Spring at mile 4.9.

Fees and permits: A reservation to park at the trailhead is highly recommended. Reservations can be made up to three months in advance by calling 723-5140 or online at baxterstateparkauthority.com.

Other maps: DeLorme's The Maine Atlas and Gazetteer maps 50 and 51.

Nat Geo TOPO! Map (USGS): Mount Katahdin and Katahdin Lake.

Nat Geo Trails Illustrated Map: Baxter State Park.

FINDING THE TRAILHEAD

From the Togue Pond Gate at the south entrance, turn right onto the Roaring Brook Road. Drive 8.0 miles to the end of the road. Hiker parking is in the lot to the left. The hike begins at the ranger station—where you need to sign in before hiking—at the north end of the parking area.
Trailhead GPS: N45° 55.180' / W68° 51.444'.

WHAT TO SEE

When most people think of Katahdin, they think of Baxter and the other peaks around the Great Basin. Everyone wants to climb Maine's highest mountain and

Looking down Hamlin Ridge
to Katahdin Lake

stand atop the iconic mountain. But, in fact, Katahdin includes the entire massif: four named basins, The Table Land, Northwest Plateau, and the North Peaks. Fewer people take the time to visit the northern reaches of Katahdin. The North Peaks hike is a good way to visit the rest of Katahdin.

You hike up the wide and busy Chimney Pond Trail almost to the campground, turning north on North Basin Trail. This trail is narrow and rougher, hemmed in by boulders and a dense forest. It's quiet and lonely.

By the time you reach Hamlin Ridge Trail, you've already climbed 1,700 feet in 3.4 miles. The Hamlin Ridge Trail climbs that much in just over a mile. As the trail climbs up slabs of pale granite, the spruce forest shrinks. Even before the trees give way entirely, you have spectacular views in every direction.

Hamlin Ridge separates North and Great Basins. On the south, the ridge drops steeply into the spruce. The forest spreads across the basin floor—mostly hiding the campground. Beyond Chimney Pond, the trees thin out and the walls of Great Basin rise to the high peaks. Voices drift across the gulf, mostly hikers celebrating summiting. To the north, Hamlin Ridge drops almost vertically into North Basin. Patches of trees grow among the broken granite, jumbled about. A figure-eight-shaped pond lays lifeless in the basin.

The trail crosses several stony knobs much like the Knife Edge, then climbs more steeply. Where you are not scrambling up boulders and slabs, you have to deal with loose gravel on the narrow trail.

Looking across the North Peaks from the shoulder of Hamlin Peak

Hamlin Peak is a flat expanse of lichen-covered rock atop high cliffs. The North Peaks are arrayed around the rim of North Basin, each slightly lower than one before it. They're all little more than piles of shifting rock—rough granite that crumbles in your hands.

Just below Hamlin Peak, at a trail junction, is Caribou Spring. A small trickle of achingly cold water flows out of the rock. Quickly, the stream is swallowed by the loose rock, but you can track its course downslope by the stand of stunted trees.

From the North Peaks, you have spectacular views of Great Basin, North Basin, Northwest Plateau, the Katahdinauguoh mountains across The Klondike, the mountains around Russell Pond and Wassataquoik Lake (both are visible), and The Traveler far to the north. It pretty much feels like you can see everything—a much more expansive view than from Baxter Peak.

For a long time, the North Peaks Trail crossed the peaks and ended at tree line north of the basin. A few years ago, the park reopened the trail beyond that—all the way to Wassataquoik Stream. You can use this route to get to or return from Russell Pond. The trail between Wassataquoik Stream and tree line where this day hike ends is a relentless climb with no views at all.

Follow the trail beyond the last North Peak as far as you like. The views are spectacular and different from those along North Basin's rim. Just remember, every step downhill you take, you'll have to undo on your return.

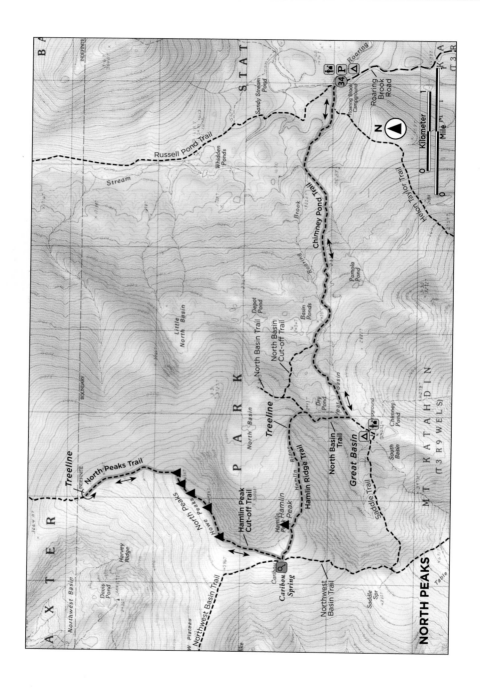

NORTH PEAKS

A reservation to park at the trailhead is highly recommended. Reservations can be made up to three months in advance by calling (207) 723–5140 or online at http://www.baxterstateparkauthority.com.

MILES AND DIRECTIONS

0.0 Start at the Roaring Brook Trailhead at the north end of the day-use parking area. In 350 feet, turn left onto Chimney Pond Trail, just before the bridge over Roaring Brook.

0.2 Pass Helon Taylor Trail.

0.8 The trail climbs gently alongside Roaring Brook. The trail leaves the stream and climbs more steeply.

1.8 A 100-foot side trail leads to a viewpoint with a great view of North Basin and Pamola Peak.

2.1 A very short side trail leads to Basin Ponds with a fine view across the pond of North Basin.

2.3 Pass North Basin Cut-off Trail. **OPTION:** You can follow North Basin Cut-off Trail to North Basin Trail to Hamlin Ridge Trail. This route is 0.4 mile shorter, but more difficult.

3.0 Turn right onto North Basin Trail.

3.4 Climb steadily to Hamlin Ridge Trail. Turn left onto it.

3.6 Climb very steeply with some rock scrambling to tree line.

4.7 The trail climbs across a series of rock knobs, then climbs very steeply with some rock scrambling and exposure to Hamlin Peak. **OPTION:** On Hamlin Peak, you can turn right onto North Peaks Trail, saving 0.2 mile. This route bypasses the only water on the mountain.

4.9 Reach Caribou Spring. Turn right onto Hamlin Peak Cut-off Trail.

5.2 Cross almost level rocky ground. Bear left onto North Peaks Trail.

5.4 Climb to the first and highest North Peak.

5.7 Cross the second peak.

5.9 Cross the third peak.

6.0 Cross the fourth peak.

6.2 Cross the last peak. **OPTION:** You can return to the trailhead from here, making the hike 12.4 miles.

7.0 The trail turns north, away from North Basin, and descends across a series of rocky knobs to tree line with spectacular views the whole way. To complete the hike, return the way you came.

14.0 Arrive back at the trailhead.

35. THE NORTH BASIN

WHY GO?

From Blueberry Knoll at the mouth of the North Basin, you have spectacular views of North Basin, Great Basin, and the country to the east. Hamlin Ridge and the Howe Peaks rise nearly vertically from North Basin. This uncrowded corner of Katahdin isn't to be missed. The hike also crosses from North Basin into Great Basin for a visit to Chimney Pond.

THE RUN DOWN

Start: From the Roaring Brook Trailhead at the north end of the day-use parking area.

Elevation gain: 1,912 feet.

Distance: 8.0 miles lollipop.

Hiking time: 4–5 hours.

Difficulty: Strenuous.

Seasons: June–Sept are best.

Trail surface: Woodland path.

Nearest town: Millinocket.

Other users: None.

Water availability: Roaring Brook, Basin Ponds, and Chimney Pond.

Fees and permits: A reservation to park at the trailhead is highly recommended. Reservations can be made up to three months in advance by calling 723-5140 or online at baxterstateparkauthority.com.

Other maps: *DeLorme's The Maine Atlas and Gazetteer* map 51.

Nat Geo TOPO! Map (USGS): Mount Katahdin and Katahdin Lake.

Nat Geo Trails Illustrated Map: Baxter State Park.

FINDING THE TRAILHEAD

From the Togue Pond Gate at the south entrance, turn right onto the Roaring Brook Road. Drive 8.0 miles to the end of the road. Hiker parking is in the lot to the left. The hike begins at the ranger station—where you need to sign in before hiking—at the north end of the parking area.
Trailhead GPS: N45° 55.180' / W68° 51.444'.

WHAT TO SEE

On most days, Katahdin's Great Basin is a buzz of activity: hikers high on the mountain shouting joyfully at their completion of the AT or just making it to Baxter Peak, campers wandering around Chimney Pond campground, and the sounds of cooking drift out from the spruce woods. Less than a mile away, the North Basin sits quiet, empty but for boulders. The view from Blueberry Knoll in North Basin

North Basin from Basin Ponds

is spectacular. There are towering cliffs, huge broken boulders, and mountains all around. The scale of it is almost beyond comprehension.

The hike follows the popular Chimney Pond Trail for a little more than 2.0 miles. At first, you follow the noisy Roaring Brook, then the trail drifts southwest and begins to climb. You are climbing up a moraine: rocky deposits left at the toe of a long-melted glacier. Near the end of the climb, a short side trail leads to an overlook with your first view of North Basin. A quarter mile later, another side trail leads to Basin Ponds. Again, you have a fine view of North Basin and Katahdin—although Pamola Peak blocks most of the mountain.

The North Basin Cut-off Trail crosses Roaring Brook—usually more rocks than water—then begins climbing toward North Basin. The trail skirts around a beaver flowage that flooded part of the trail. Stay to the left just above the water and you'll be back on the trail in no time.

Past the flooded section, the trail climbs more steeply. The trailbed is boulders and bedrock. There are occasional views behind you of Basin Ponds. On a level shelf, the cutoff ends at North Basin Trail. You turn right and climb again. As you near Blueberry Knoll, the trees shrink and the vista opens. High cliffs arch around you, topped by Howe and Hamlin Peaks. To the south, past the jagged line of Hamlin Ridge, is the Great Basin and the ring of Katahdin's highest peaks.

Higher in North Basin is a small pond that you can bushwhack to. But remember that North Basin is much larger than it appears. The pond is nestled behind a sprucy ridge that looks 10 minutes away, but it's much farther.

You could return the way you came to the trailhead, but go ahead and hike over to Great Basin. Stand on the shore of Chimney Pond and crane your neck up at the peaks. Watch the hikers like fleas make their way across the Knife Edge. With your eyes, trace the line of granite known as The Cathedral. This is Pamola's home, the legendary half eagle, half moose beast that creates the weather. Leroy Dudley, who built the first ranger's cabin at Chimney Pond, befriended Pamola. He spent his days guiding folks up the mountain and telling tales about his friend.

Before heading back to the trailhead, spend a moment to consider the different experiences of standing in North and Great Basins. They're very different. Neither is to be missed.

A reservation to park at the trailhead is highly recommended. Reservations can be made up to three months in advance by calling (207) 723-5140 or online at http://www.baxterstateparkauthority.com.

MILES AND DIRECTIONS

0.0 Start from the Roaring Brook Trailhead at the north end of the day-use parking area. After 350 feet, turn left staying on Chimney Pond Trail.

0.2 Pass Helon Taylor Trail.

0.8 The trail climbs gently alongside Roaring Brook. The trail leaves the stream and climbs more steeply.

1.8 A 100-foot side trail leads to a viewpoint with a great view of North Basin and Pamola Peak.

2.1 A very short side trail leads to Basin Ponds with fine views across the pond.

2.5 The trail slabs around the pond, then climbs. Turn right onto the North Basin Cut-off Trail.

2.8 The trail becomes obscured by a beaver flowage. Stay to the left and work your way around the flooded trail.

3.2 Beyond the beaver flowage, the trail climbs steeply. Turn right onto the North Basin Trail.

3.5 The trail climbs to the top of Blueberry Knoll at the mouth of North Basin. To continue your hike, return to the junction with the North Basin Cut-off Trail.

3.8 Pass the North Basin Cut-off Trail.

4.1 Pass the Hamlin Ridge Trail.

4.5 Turn right onto Chimney Pond Trail.

4.7 Climb to Chimney Pond campground. Follow the trail through the campground to the ranger's station. Pass the ranger's station and the Dudley Trail, Chimney Pond is 150 feet farther. To complete your hike, follow Chimney Pond Trail all the way back to the trailhead.

8.0 Arrive back at the trailhead.

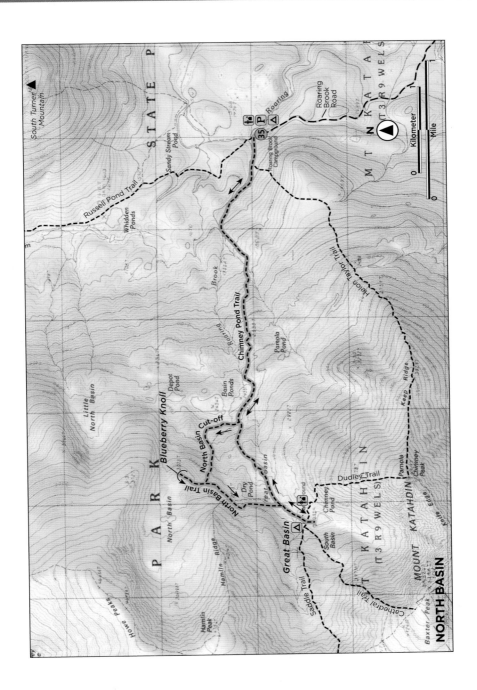

36. KATAHDIN VIA THE KNIFE EDGE

WHY GO?

This is the classic hike. There's no hike more iconic in Maine. The route climbs Keep Ridge with fine views to Pamola Peak. You then descend into and climb right out of The Chimney. The Knife Edge begins as you cross Chimney Peak. The trail crosses over and around a series of serrated knobs that drop dramatically into Great Basin. An exhilarating climb brings you to Baxter Peak, the highest point in Maine and the northern terminus of the Appalachian Trail. From there, the hike descends into The Saddle with fine views in every direction. The Saddle Trail then drops steeply down a slide, leading toward Chimney Pond. From Chimney Pond, it's a little more than a 3-mile descent to the trailhead.

THE RUN DOWN

Start: From the Roaring Brook ranger station at the north end of the parking area.

Elevation gain: 4,152 feet.

Distance: 9.6 miles loop.

Hiking time: 8–10 hours.

Difficulty: Most strenuous.

Seasons: July–Sept are best.

Trail surface: Woodland path and granite bedrock.

Nearest town: Millinocket.

Other users: None.

Water availability: Bear Brook at mile 1.4 and a small stream at mile 5.5.

Fees and permits: A reservation to park at the trailhead is highly recommended. Reservations can be made up to three months in advance by calling 723-5140 or online at baxterstateparkauthority.com.

Other maps: *DeLorme's The Maine Atlas and Gazetteer* maps 50 and 51.

Nat Geo TOPO! Map (USGS): Katahdin Lake.

Nat Geo Trails Illustrated Map: Baxter State Park.

FINDING THE TRAILHEAD

From the Togue Pond Gate at the south entrance, turn right onto the Roaring Brook Road. Drive 8.0 miles to the end of the road. Hiker parking is in the lot to the left. The hike begins at the ranger station—where you need to sign in before hiking—at the north end of the parking area.
Trailhead GPS: N45° 55.180' / W68° 51.444'.

Chimney Pond in the Great Basin
surrounded by Katahdin's highest peaks

WHAT TO SEE

Katahdin creates its own weather, and is often capped by a cloud even on clear days. It can snow on any day of the year and is usually windy above tree line. Hikers should be prepared: Don't wear cotton clothing, bring a hat and a coat, and pack plenty of water and snacks. Remember that nearly half the hike is above tree line, exposed to the weather. Most importantly, take your time and respect the mountain. The earlier in the day you begin your hike the better. It's not uncommon to see hikers arriving at the trailhead before it's even light. You don't need to start that early, but it's best to be on the trail by 7 or 8 a.m.

Because this is such a popular route up Katahdin, it's recommended that you make a trailhead parking reservation. Reservations can be made by calling (207) 723-5140 or online at http://www.baxterstateparkauthority.com. The park will only hold your parking spot until 7:05 a.m. It's their way of encouraging hikers to get an early start.

The hike begins climbing almost immediately. After all, you begin at an elevation of just over 1,500 feet, and Pamola Peak, the first peak you reach, is 4,919 feet. That's a lot of climbing in 3.2 miles. As you climb toward the tree line, you have to scale several small rock faces and pass overlooks with views to the east and north. The higher you climb, more of the surrounding country emerges. By the time you reach the tree line, you can see the Turner Mountains to the northeast with The Traveler beyond them. To the east is Katahdin Lake, surrounded by an endless forest. To the

The Knife Edge

northwest, you can see right into North Basin with its dramatic cliffs that rise to Hamlin and Howe Peaks. The peaks of the North Basin are part of Katahdin. The mountain encompasses not just the peaks around Great Basin and the Table Land, but also the North Peaks, the North, and Northwest Basins.

The trail follows the spine of Keep Ridge toward Pamola Peak, steepening as you climb. The north ridge of Pamola Peak begins to block the view northwest, but the arc of the Knife Edge comes into view. Before the final push to the summit, you get a view right through The Chimney. Pamola Peak sits right on the edge of Great Basin, and Baxter Peak directly across the great yawning gulf. The jagged arc of the Knife Edge connects the two. To the northwest, North Basin has come back into view. Beyond it, across a wide swath of tableland is the little-visited Northwest Basin. In the distance, you can see The Brothers, Mount O-J-I, and behind them

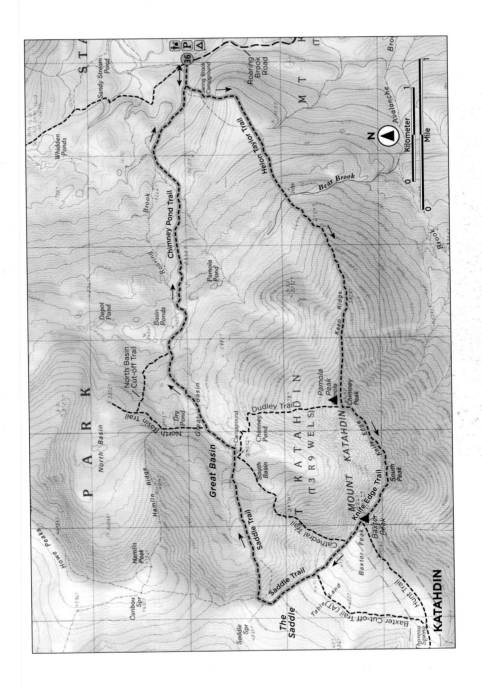

Doubletop Mountain. Pamola Peak itself seems to be little more than a pile of loose granite mottled with lichen.

The descent from Pamola Peak into The Chimney, and then the climb to Chimney Peak, is the most technically difficult section of the entire hike. The trail drops 100 feet of elevation in only 260 feet of trail. The climb up to Chimney Peak is almost as steep. The Knife Edge itself begins as you descend off Chimney Peak. The trail winds over and around a series of serrated ridges that drop dramatically into Great Basin. More than a 1,000 feet below you, Chimney Pond looks like a small puddle.

Baxter Peak is 5,267 feet—13 feet short of a mile. There's a large cairn on the summit that makes the mountain a mile-high. Near the cairn is the sign denoting the northern end of the Appalachian Trail. Thru-hikers and day hikers alike queue up to get their picture taken celebrating at the sign. Their whoops can be heard all across Katahdin and even down at Chimney Pond.

The hike follows the Saddle Trail off the summit down into The Saddle. As you descend, you can see the orangish gash of a slide where the Saddle Trail drops down toward Chimney Pond. The trail is extremely steep and descends loose rock. Take your time and enjoy the view of Katahdin as you carefully descend. Even after the trail turns to bedrock and you enter the trees, the trail drops and drops. Then, suddenly, you reach the ranger's station on the shore of Chimney Pond. It was here that Leroy Dudley was ranger for years, entertaining hikers and campers with yarns of Pamola—the mythological creature who lived atop Katahdin and controlled the weather. He was, according to the Penobscots, a giant with a moose's head and an eagle's legs and wings. It was respect for his power that kept Penobscots from climbing the mountain.

Before heading down the Chimney Pond Trail to the trailhead, walk out to the shore of Chimney Pond. You can see the jagged line from Pamola Peak across the Knife Edge to Baxter Peak that you hiked. Even as you hear voices drifting down from above, the scale of the mountain renders the scene almost unreal. But your sore feet and legs know all too well that it was real. You have more than 3.0 miles to hike back to the trailhead, so don't linger too long.

MILES AND DIRECTIONS

0.0 Start from the Roaring Brook ranger's station at the north end of the parking area. Be sure to sign in on the front porch of the ranger's station.

400 feet Pass the Russell Pond Trail that crosses Roaring Brook within sight of the junction.

0.2 Turn left onto the Helon Taylor Trail.

1.4 The trail crosses Bear Brook.

2.2 The trail reaches the tree line with views ahead to Pamola Peak and into North Basin. As the trail climbs, you get views of the Knife Edge and Chimney Peak.

3.2 Reach Pamola Peak. Turn left onto the Knife Edge Trail.

3.3 The Knife Edge Trail descends very steeply into The Chimney, losing 100 feet of elevation in less than 260 feet of trail. From The Chimney, the trail climbs Chimney Peak, gaining almost 100 feet in less than 500 feet of trail. This is the toughest section of trail on the entire hike.

4.0 The trail crosses the Knife Edge to unmarked South Peak.

4.3 The trail climbs from South Peak to Baxter Peak, the highest point in Maine and the northern terminus of the Appalachian Trail. From the summit, descend into The Saddle on the Saddle Trail.

4.5 Pass the Cathedral Trail. This trail descends to Chimney Pond in 1.6 miles—a shorter but more difficult descent.

4.8 Pass the Cathedral Cut-off Trail.

5.2 Junction with the Northwest Basin Trail in The Saddle. The Saddle Trail descends a steep slide to the east from The Saddle. The Northwest Basin Trail climbs out of The Saddle toward Hamlin and Howe Peaks, then on to Northwest Basin.

5.5 The Saddle Trail descends steeply to tree line with views across the Great Basin. Into the trees, the trail descends to a small stream.

6.2 Pass the Cathedral Trail.

6.3 Arrive at the Chimney Pond ranger's station. Turn left onto the Chimney Pond Trail east toward Roaring Brook. A short side trail leads to the right to Chimney Pond.

6.4 Arrive at Chimney Pond.

6.7 Pass the North Basin Trail.

7.3 Pass the North Basin Cut-off Trail.

7.7 A short side trail leads 100 feet to Basin Ponds, the source of Roaring Brook.

9.6 Arrive back at the trailhead. Be sure to sign out on the front porch of the ranger's station.

37. ROARING BROOK NATURE TRAIL

WHY GO?
Roaring Brook Nature Trail is a short loop through the woods across Roaring Brook from the campground. The trail skirts the edge of a good-sized raised peat bog. You can find pitcher plants and sundews growing in the sphagnum moss. From two bog board viewpoints, you have fine views of South Turner Mountain and Katahdin.

THE RUN DOWN

Start: From the Roaring Brook Trailhead at the north end of the day-use parking area.

Elevation gain: 119 feet.

Distance: 1.2 miles lollipop.

Hiking time: About 1 hour.

Difficulty: Easy.

Seasons: May–Oct are best.

Trail surface: Woodland path.

Nearest town: Millinocket.

Other users: None.

Water availability: Roaring Brook, near the trailhead.

Fees and permits: A reservation to park at the trailhead is highly recommended. Reservations can be made up to three months in advance by calling 723-5140 or online at baxterstateparkauthority.com.

Other maps: *DeLorme's The Maine Atlas and Gazetteer* map 51.

Nat Geo TOPO! Map (USGS): Katahdin Lake.

Nat Geo Trails Illustrated Map: Baxter State Park.

FINDING THE TRAILHEAD
From the Togue Pond Gate at the south entrance, turn right onto the Roaring Brook Road. Drive 8.0 miles to the end of the road. Hiker parking is in the lot to the left. The hike begins at the ranger station—where you need to sign in before hiking—at the north end of the parking area.
Trailhead GPS: N45° 55.180' / W68° 51.444'.

WHAT TO SEE
From high on Baxter's many mountains, you can look out across the forested country and see ponds, streams, and treeless areas that shine emerald green in the sunlight. These green areas are raised peat bogs. You could walk past one on a trail—a 100 feet through the woods—and never know it. Roaring Brook Nature Trail visits one.

The trail begins across Roaring Brook from the campground. It follows downstream for a couple hundred yards before turning into the woods and crossing a low,

South Turner Mountain from the first bog boardwalk

swampy area. You cross through a spruce forest full of mossy rocks, and, where the ground is highest, abundant wildflowers.

The trail turns north and reaches the edge of a good-sized peat bog. A short boardwalk, sunken into the thick sphagnum moss, leads to a viewpoint. Across the bog, South Turner Mountain rises with its prominent rocky summit. Turn left to the west and you have a fine view of Katahdin. From this perspective, Pamola Peak and North Basin dominate.

Take time to look down at the mat of moss. Dozens of different kinds of plants grow in and through it. Two of the most interesting are pitcher plants and sundews. Both are carnivorous. The acid, almost soilless conditions required the ancient forebears of these plants to find another way to get the nutrients they needed. They catch insects. The pitcher plants drown them in their cuplike leaves; the sundews trap them on their sticky leaves with tiny drops of a honey-like substance.

The trail skirts along the edge of the bog to another viewpoint before angling back toward Roaring Brook.

A reservation to park at the trailhead is highly recommended. Reservations can be made up to three months in advance by calling (207) 723-5140 or online at http://www.baxterstateparkauthority.com.

Katahdin from the first
bog boardwalk

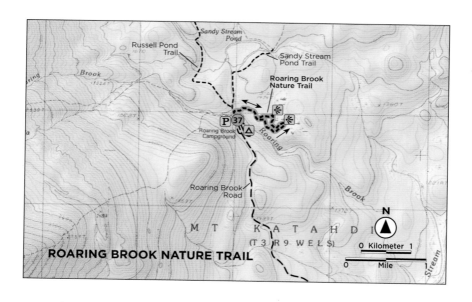

ROARING BROOK NATURE TRAIL

MILES AND DIRECTIONS

0.0 Start from the Roaring Brook Trailhead at the north end of the day-use parking area.

0.1 Pass the ranger's station, then in 350 feet pass Chimney Pond Trail. Go straight across the bridge over Roaring Brook onto the Russell Pond Trail. Immediately across the bridge, turn right onto the Roaring Brook Nature Trail.

0.3 The trail follows Roaring Brook, then turns into the woods and crosses a low, swampy area. Bear right at the fork.

0.6 Reach at the first bog boardwalk viewpoint.

0.7 Reach at the second bog boardwalk viewpoint.

0.9 Arrive back at the fork. Turn right and retrace your steps to the trailhead.

1.2 Arrive back at the trailhead.

BACKPACKING TRIPS

Young backpacker on Wadleigh Brook Trail

38. NORTHWEST BASIN

WHY GO?

The Northwest Basin, one of Katahdin's three basins, is surrounded by towering cliffs and rugged mountains. It takes two days to get there. The first is an easy hike to Russell Pond. The second, a shorter but more challenging hike to Davis Pond in the heart of the basin. Following the Northwest Basin Trail over Northwest Plateau and then hiking down Hamlin Ridge makes the three-day trip a loop. This challenging hike visits some of Baxter's more remote and spectacular scenery.

THE RUN DOWN

Start: From the Roaring Brook Trailhead at the north end of parking area.

Elevation gain: 5,142 (1,066, 2,076, and 2,000) feet.

Distance: 22.5 (8.1, 6.3, and 8.1) miles loop.

Hiking time: 3 days.

Difficulty: Most strenuous.

Seasons: July–Sept are best.

Trail surface: Woodland path and mountain top.

Nearest town: Millinocket.

Other users: None.

Water availability: See Miles and Description.

Other maps: *DeLorme's The Maine Atlas and Gazetteer* map 50.

Nat Geo TOPO! Map (USGS): Mount Katahdin and Katahdin Lake.

Nat Geo Trails Illustrated Map: Baxter State Park.

FINDING THE TRAILHEAD

From the Togue Pond Gate, turn right onto the Roaring Brook Road. Drive 8.0 miles to the end of the road. Backpacker parking is in the lot to the right. The hike begins at the ranger station—where you need to sign in before hiking—at the north end of the parking area.
Trailhead GPS: N45° 55.180' / W68° 51.444'.

WHAT TO SEE

Katahdin has three major glacial-carved basins: Great, North, and Northwest. The Northwest Basin is the most remote and least visited. The cliffs that arc around the basin are among the highest in the park, rising nearly vertically almost 1,000 feet. Ribbons of water crash down their face, filling Davis Pond. From atop the moraine at the mouth of Northwest Basin, you have an incredible view of the basin and the mountains to the north and across The Klondike.

Davis Pond nestled high in Northwest Basin seen from the North Brother

To get to Northwest Basin takes two days. First, you follow Russell Pond Trail north from Roaring Brook. The relatively flat trail follows the south branch of Wassataquoik Stream from Whidden Ponds, where you have a spectacular view of Katahdin. Past Wassataquoik Stream Trail, you cross the stream and slab around the eastern flank of Russell Mountain.

You have to ford Wassataquoik Stream—a wide, rocky river. In the spring or during a rainy year, this crossing can be dangerous: Exercise caution. Across the stream, you pass through the site of New City before reaching Russell Pond.

From Russell Pond, the second day, you follow an old road up Wassataquoik Valley. The trail climbs very little. As you near Wassataquoik Stream, the trail becomes rockier. You need to ford Annis Brook. Take a snack break and explore Annis Brook from the trail down to Wassataquoik Stream. Giant boulders litter the streambed, some as large as cabins. The water crashes through the boulder field; mountains rise steeply from the stream. All morning, you've been hiking into a narrowing valley.

Farther on, the trail comes into a small glen. Gravelly cliffs rise steeply up Mullen Mountain. To the south, Wassataquoik Stream pours out of a narrow cleft between Fort Mountain and the northern-most arm of Katahdin. The glen is green and lush. It seems like the ideal spot for a hermit's cabin, but only beavers live here.

The Northwest Plateau from
above Caribou Spring

The trail crosses the shallow stream and enters the woods. This section of trail is often flooded, but with care you can keep your feet dry. As you pass between the mountains, the trail climbs gently along a small stream. You come to an extensive slab of exposed bedrock with water running down it. The trail climbs the rock, then climbs steeply toward Northwest Basin. This trail, too, is often very wet. There has been talk of rerouting the trail away from the water, but the park is convinced that wherever they put this trail, the water will find it. So, plan to have wet feet. This section is very steep.

The trail tops out on a knoll above Cowles Lake. You are now in Northwest Basin. The trail crosses semi-open ground into the basin. Huge boulders sit here and there. You are surrounded by towering cliffs.

The Davis Pond lean-to is on the forested slope down to the pond. Because of the fragile nature of this remote area, no fires are allowed at the lean-to. Exploring around the pond is rewarding, but challenging. Dense shrubs and alders crowd the pond. The floor of the pond is vegetation kept too cold to fully decompose. Near the head of the outlet stream, there are a few tub-sized pools you can cool off in.

The last day is a spectacular hike up to and over Northwest Plateau. From Davis Pond, you climb relentlessly—at first through forested slope, then up a rocky slide. The Northwest Plateau is a great expanse of tundra that stretches in undulations toward Katahdin's high peaks. All around you, the world drops away in nearly sheer cliffs. Across green valleys, rise rugged peaks. This feels like Alaska, not Maine.

Where the plateau begins to rise to Hamlin Peak, you reach Caribou Spring and Hamlin Ridge Trail. Cross Hamlin Peak, little more than a rocky bump with fine views in every direction. Don't spend all your time staring open-mouthed into Great Basin. Turn in each direction and take in all the view.

Hamlin Ridge Trail descends the narrow ridge, often hugging the edge of the 1,000-foot cliff. In many ways, this descent is more challenging and more exposed than the infamous Knife Edge. The trail drops relentlessly, often down huge boulders and over gravel-covered bedrock. Eventually, you drop into the forest still descending steeply.

The trail ends at North Basin Trail. Turn right and head toward Chimney Pond. It's shorter to turn left and take the North Basin Cut-off Trail, but that way is more difficult. You can hike on back to the trailhead, or spend a night at Chimney Pond. You've come less than 5.0 miles from Davis Pond, but it feels like much more. Know your limits and plan accordingly.

Backcountry camping fees and permit required. Non-Maine residents also pay an auto entrance fee.

Turner Deadwater near Russell Pond on Northwest Basin Trail

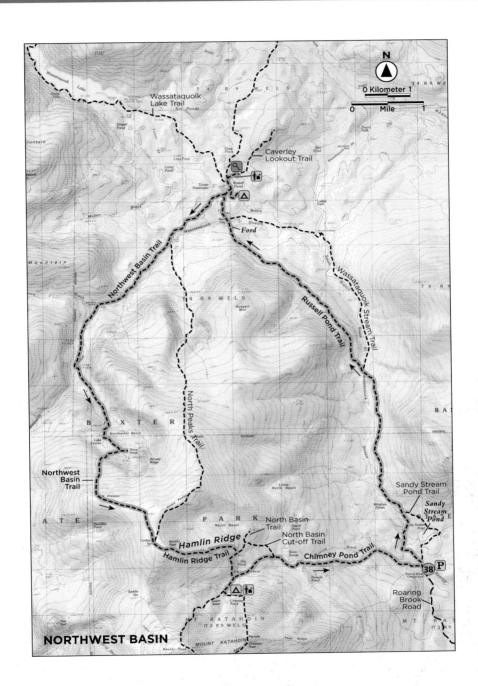

N

0 Kilometer 1

0 Mile 1

Wassataquoik Lake Trail

Caverley Lookout Trail

Northwest Basin Trail

Ford

Russell Pond Trail

Wassataquoik Stream Trail

North Peaks Trail

Northwest Basin Trail

Sandy Stream Pond Trail

Sandy Stream Pond

Hamlin Ridge

North Basin Trail

North Basin Cut-off Trail

Hamlin Ridge Trail

Chimney Pond Trail

38

Roaring Brook Road

NORTHWEST BASIN

MILES AND DIRECTIONS

DAY 1

0.0 Start from the Roaring Brook Trailhead at the north end of the parking area.

0.1 Turn right onto the Russell Pond Trail, crossing Roaring Brook. Across the bridge, pass Sandy Stream Pond Trail.

1.2 Pass Sandy Stream Pond Trail.

1.4 A short side trail on the left leads to Whidden Pond with a spectacular view of Katahdin.

3.4 Turn left, passing Wassataquoik Stream Trail.

7.2 Ford Wassataquoik Stream.

7.6 Pass Wassataquoik Stream Trail.

7.8 Pass Northwest Basin Trail.

7.9 Reach Russell Pond.

8.1 The trail goes around the pond to where the ranger's station is on the north shore of Russell Pond.

DAY 2

0.0 From Russell Pond Trail, turn right onto Northwest Basin Trail.

0.2 Cross Turner Stream just below the deadwater.

1.2 Pass North Peaks Trail.

2.6 Cross Annis Brook.

4.2 Ford Wassataquoik Stream.

5.6 Climb very steeply to a rocky knoll above Lake Cowles.

6.3 Cross an open ridge in the heart of the Northwest Basin, then descend to Davis Pond lean-to. A short side trail leads down to the pond.

DAY 3

0.0 The Northwest Basin Trail drops down past the Davis Pond lean-to, then climbs very steeply.

1.3 At the top of a large rock slide, reach the Northwest Plateau.

2.4 Cross the plateau to Caribou Spring. Turn left onto the Hamlin Ridge Trail.

2.7 Cross Hamlin Peak.

4.0 Steeply descend the narrow Hamlin Ridge. Turn right onto the North Basin Trail.

4.3 Turn right onto the Chimney Pond Trail.

4.8 Reach Chimney Pond. To complete the hike, follow the Chimney Pond Trail back to Roaring Brook Trailhead. **OPTION:** You can add a day to the hike and camp at Chimney Pond.

8.1 The Chimney Pond Trail descends past the Basin Ponds, then along Roaring Brook to the Roaring Brook Trailhead.

39. KATAHDIN LAKE

WHY GO?

The view of Katahdin from the south shore of Katahdin Lake was made famous by painters Frederic Church and, especially, Marsden Hartley. You get that iconic view before lunch the first day. Then it's easy miles to the north shore of the lake. The day hike to Twin Ponds involves a climb, but isn't hard. The ponds sit in a small basin surrounded by North Turner Mountain. On the return trip, you visit Martin Ponds and see another spectacular view of Katahdin. All along this three-day trip are great opportunities for wildlife viewing.

THE RUN DOWN

Start: From the Katahdin Lake Trailhead across Roaring Brook Road from the Avalanche Field parking area.

Elevation gain: 2,722 (726, 1,201, and 795) feet.

Distance: 19.6 (7.4, 7.4, and 4.8) miles out and back.

Hiking time: 3 days.

Difficulty: Moderate.

Seasons: June–Sept are best.

Trail surface: Woodland path.

Nearest town: Millinocket.

Other users: None.

Water availability: See Miles and Description.

Fees and permits: Backcountry camping fees and permit required. Non-Maine residents also pay an auto entrance fee.

Other maps: DeLorme's The Maine Atlas and Gazetteer map.

Nat Geo TOPO! Map (USGS): Katahdin Lake.

Nat Geo Trails Illustrated Map: Baxter State Park.

FINDING THE TRAILHEAD

From the Togue Pond Gate at the south entrance, turn right onto the Roaring Brook Road. Drive 6.5 miles. The Avalanche Field parking area is on the left. The trailhead is across Roaring Brook Road. Trailhead GPS: N45° 54.136' / W68° 50.550'.

WHAT TO SEE

In 1848, Marcus Keep cut a trail from Wassataquoik Stream to Katahdin Lake and onto Katahdin. The trail climbed the ridge to Pamola Peak that now bears his name. This was the first hiking trail cut to and on Katahdin. Previous climbs of Katahdin, like Thoreau's in 1846, were from the south, but no actual trail was ever cut.

The famous view of Katahdin from South Katahdin Lake day-use area

Keep's trail was in common use until the 1870s, when it was obliterated by heavy logging. A new trail was cut that ended in Great Basin. After that, various plans to build a road to Chimney Pond, passing the south shore of Katahdin Lake came and went.

By the late 1880s, a commercial camp was on the south shore of Katahdin Lake, where it remains today. To get there, guests followed a trail from the Wassataquoik to the north shore of Katahdin Lake. They were ferried across the lake by boat to the camps. The camps went through several owners over the years. In the twentieth century, access to the camps was from Avalanche Field via a buckboard road. This is the route of today's Katahdin Lake Trail.

Katahdin Lake attracted attention not just because of the early access it afforded to Katahdin, but also for moose hunting, trout fishing, and the spectacular scenery. Artists including Frederic Church and Marsden Hartley came to paint the view of Katahdin across the lake.

Percival Baxter always regretted that he was unable to add Katahdin Lake to Baxter State Park. In 2006, after long negotiations involving the state, logging companies, several nonprofits, and a complex land swap, Katahdin Lake was added to Baxter State Park.

The trail from Avalanche Field descends gently to a bridge over Sandy Stream just below its confluence with Roaring Brook. From Sandy Stream, it crosses a small knoll, then gently descends to the south shore of Katahdin Lake. The trail

North Turner Mountain across the smaller of the Twin Ponds

continues past the commercial camps to the eastern boundary of the park where it becomes the International Appalachian Trail. Before the camps the hike turns down a side trail that leads to the South Katahdin Lake lean-to and a picnic area. There are rental canoes at each site. The view of Katahdin here is quite famous. Watch for loons and their nests on the nearby island.

From the lake, follow Martin Ponds Trail north along the shore. You have to ford the sandy inlet where Martin Ponds Stream drains into the lake. Sun fish make their nests in the gravel on the bottom. You need to ford the shallow stream and follow the shore of the lake north. The trail reenters the woods and follows the lake shore before angling northwest and climbing gently.

The North Katahdin Lake Trail slabs around the shoulder of South Turner Mountain. There's very little elevation change before reaching the North Katahdin Lake lean-to. You can't see Katahdin from the shore, but by paddling the provided canoe to the west side of the lake you do. Watch for eagles on the lake. Also, near the north shore of the lake, in a large white pine, is a raven's nest. During midsummer, suckers can be seen migrating from the lake up into the small streams where they breed.

The second day is a day hike up to Twin Ponds and back to North Katahdin Lake lean-to. The trail loops around East Turner Mountain, leaving the park. About a mile from the lean-to, the trail passes through a boulder field. There's a small ice cave under the boulders. A hiker can just squeeze into the space and drop 10 feet into the cool cave.

The trail turns northwest and begins to climb gently. You cross several rocky, dry outflow channels that drain Twin Ponds. You reenter Baxter State Park and begin climbing steeply. The forest transitions from hardwoods to evergreens and the way becomes more rocky.

The first Twin Pond is a shallow, rock-lined bowl that varies in size from year to year, depending on how much it snows. Untrailed North Turner Mountain rises just to the north. Its summit is a bare rocky cap.

The trail reenters the woods, then ends at the south shore of the larger Twin Pond. Across the pond, the steep slopes of North Turner Mountain rise with areas of bare rock. The cold water of the pond is home to beautiful brook trout—many stocked here a hundred years ago from Katahdin Lake. The dense growth around the pond and marshy ground between the two ponds make it nearly impossible to explore around the pond. Enjoy a swim and lunch at the trail's end before returning to Katahdin Lake.

The third day is the shortest. The return route takes the short cut to Martin Ponds. The Martin Ponds Trail descends from its junction with North Katahdin Lake Trail to loop around the smaller of the two Martin Ponds. This first pond is marshy and a good

Katahdin across Martin Pond

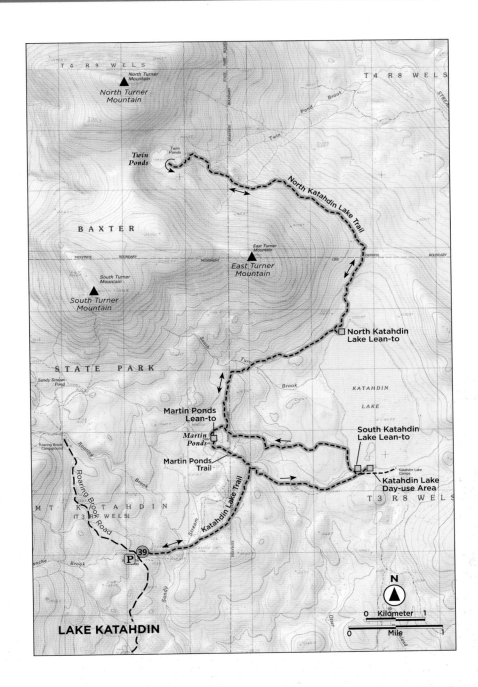

moose habitat. A short side trail leads to the lean-to on the larger Martin Pond. The view from the small dock provided to launch the canoe isn't to be missed. Katahdin rises dramatically across the marshy pond. From this eastern view, Pamola Peak and the North Basin dominate. It's very similar—only closer—to the view made famous by Hartley's paintings. Be sure to watch for moose and ducks in the pond.

From Martin Pond, it's an easy hike over a small hill to Katahdin Lake Trail. This trip is a relatively easy three days. There are great opportunities for seeing wildlife and little chance of encountering other hikers once you leave Katahdin Lake Trail.

Backcountry camping fees and permit required. Non-Maine residents also pay an auto entrance fee.

MILES AND DIRECTIONS

DAY 1

0.0   Start from the Katahdin Lake Trailhead, across Roaring Brook Road from the Avalanche Field parking area.

0.5   Cross Sandy Stream.

1.7   Pass Martin Ponds Trail.

2.9   Pass the other end of Martin Ponds Trail.

3.0   Pass South Katahdin Lake lean-to.

3.1   Reach Katahdin Lake day-use area. To continue the hike, return to Martin Ponds Trail.

3.3   Turn right onto Martin Ponds Trail.

3.5   The trail appears to end on a sandy beach. Ford the inlet and hike up Katahdin Lake's shore 100 feet to the trail.

3.8   The trail bends away from Katahdin Lake and begins to climb gently.

5.3   Turn right onto North Katahdin Lake Trail.

6.2   Cross a stream.

7.3   Turn right on the side trail to North Katahdin Lake lean-to.

7.6   Arrive at the lean-to.

DAY 2

0.0   Start from the North Katahdin Lake lean-to. Hike to the North Katahdin Lake Trail.

0.1   Turn right onto the North Katahdin Lake Trail.

0.2   Pass the lake access trail. In 300 feet, cross a small stream.

1.0   Pass a cave under boulders on the left side of the trail.

3.6 The trail climbs gently, then more steeply to the first Twin Pond.

3.7 Pass around the west side of the first pond and reenter the woods to the second, larger Twin Pond. To complete the hike, return the way you came.

7.4 Arrive back at North Katahdin Lake lean-to.

DAY 3

0.0 From North Katahdin Lake lean-to, return to North Katahdin Lake Trail.

0.1 Turn left on North Katahdin Lake Trail.

2.1 Turn right onto Martin Ponds Trail.

2.3 Loop around the first Martin Pond.

2.4 Turn right onto the side trail to Martin Pond lean-to. Reach Martin Pond in 100 feet. To continue the hike, return to Martin Ponds Trail and turn right.

3.1 Arrive back at Katahdin Lake Trail. Turn right to return to the trailhead.

4.8 Arrive back at the trailhead.

40. **RUSSELL POND**

WHY GO?

Russell Pond is a backcountry campground in the Wassataquoik Valley in the center of Baxter State Park. The hike to Russell Pond is relatively flat, but interesting. From Russell Pond, you can day hike to Wassataquoik Lake, Deep Pond, Caverly Lookout (the only climb on this four day trip), Grand Falls, Ledge Falls, and Russell Pond itself. There are rental canoes at several places and good swimming at several others. The area is good for wildlife viewing, especially moose. In mid-to-late summer, blueberries line many of the trails.

THE RUN DOWN

Start: From the Roaring Brook Trailhead at the north end of the day-use parking area.

Elevation gain: 4,390 (675, 1,232, 1,154, and 1,329) feet.

Distance: 29.1 (7.8, 5.3, 8.7, and 7.3) miles.

Hiking time: 4 days.

Difficulty: Moderate.

Seasons: July–Sept are best.

Trail surface: Woodland path.

Nearest town: Millinocket.

Other users: None.

Water availability: Many.

Other maps: *DeLorme's The Maine Atlas and Gazetteer* maps 50 and 51.

Nat Geo TOPO! Map (USGS): Mount Katahdin, Katahdin Lake, Wassataquoik Lake, and The Traveler.

Nat Geo Trails Illustrated Map: Baxter State Park.

FINDING THE TRAILHEAD

From the Togue Pond Gate at the south entrance, turn right onto the Roaring Brook Road. Drive 8.0 miles to the end of the road. Hiker parking is in the lot to the left. The hike begins at the ranger station—where you need to sign in before hiking—at the north end of the parking area.
Trailhead GPS: N45° 55.180' / W68° 51.444'.

WHAT TO SEE

Wassataquoik Stream rises in The Klondike, the high swampy plateau between Katahdin and the Katahdinauguoh mountains. It flows northeast between towering mountains into a wide, flat valley. Ponds and bogs interrupt the valley's forest. Numerous streams drain the surrounding mountains. The most important of these,

North and South Turner
from the ranger's dock
on Russell Pond

Turner Brook, flows from Wassataquoik Lake through a series of ponds and dead-waters to Wassataquoik Stream southeast of Russell Pond. It's very mossy country.

The mountains around the valley are all untrailed: North Turner, Russell, Mullen, Wassataquoik, South Pogy, North Pogy, South Traveler, and Sable Mountains. The Pogy Mountains are the most remote place east of the Mississippi River.

Ironically, this part of Baxter State Park may have been the most intensively used and altered by logging. In 1858, the Wassataquoik Valley was called New England's last wilderness. Selective logging had been going on for years, mostly for white pine. Adventurers and climbers began using the logging roads to access the region and climb Katahdin from the north.

Things changed on October 16, 1883, when the Tracy-Love logging operation began. The date is certain because it's etched onto the side of Inscription Rock, a huge boulder sitting in Wassataquoik Stream above Grand Falls. The loggers felled trees, built numerous dams, and built an extensive logging camp just east of today's park boundary.

A major forest fire in 1903 destroyed the logging camp and stopped work for a time. Eventually, the camp was rebuilt as New City farther upstream. More roads were pushed up the valleys of Wassataquoik Stream and its tributaries. Many of the roadbeds are today's trails. Dams were built to allow logs to be run down the steep, rocky streams. An even more extensive fire in 1915 brought logging in Wassataquoik Valley to an end.

Even today, as you hike around the valley, you can find evidence of the fires and logging. Iron tools and wire lay here and there, rusting into the ground. Hay meadow have become alder breaks. Impoundments behind dams have become bogs or meadows. Where Wassataquoik Stream Trail passes through the site of New City, most of the trees are about the same age—a phenomenon found in spots all across central Baxter State Park. It's ironic that today's remote wilderness grew out of one of the more destructive logging eras in Maine's history.

Russell Pond is the epicenter of the valley today. There's a campground with lean-tos, tent sites, and a bunkhouse. Trails ray out in every direction. There are three basic ways to hike into Russell Pond:

1. You can hike in from the north on Pogy Notch Trail. It's 8.7 miles from Lower South Branch Pond to Russell Pond. The hiking is relatively easy and there are no challenging stream fords.
2. You can hike in from the west on Wassataquoik Lake Trail. It's 16.7 miles from Nesowadnehunk Field to Russell Pond. This is the longest route and the only one that involves climbing. Sections are very wet, overgrown, or obscured by blowdowns. Its advantages are that it passes through very remote, little-visited country and passes Wassataquoik Lake.
3. You can hike in from the south on Russell Pond Trail. It's 7.2 miles from Roaring Brook Trailhead to Russell Pond. This is the shortest and most-used route. Its disadvantages are that it's not very interesting and involves a sometimes dangerous ford of Wassataquoik Stream.

The route followed by this hike is a modification of the Russell Pond Trail route, adjusted to deal with both of its downsides.

In addition, Northwest Basin and North Peaks Trails can be used to access Russell Pond. Both trails begin up on Katahdin and end just south of Russell Pond. Rather than use them to get to Russell Pond, hike them separately (see North Peaks and Northwest Basin).

When you visit Russell Pond, use this hike as a guide not a rule. If you want to fish, spend more time at the various ponds, or stay a night at one of the outlying lean-tos (Wassataquoik Island, Wassataquoik Lake, Wassataquoik Stream, and Pogy Pond), or schedule in time for swimming, moose watching, or blueberrying.

The Russell Pond Trailhead is north from Roaring Brook. There's little elevation change on the entire first day. Be sure to stop at Whidden Ponds. There's a fine view of Katahdin across the pond. This pond is the source of South Branch of Wassataquoik Stream.

The trail roughly follows the stream, usually on a sidehill above it. Where the trail comes within sight of the stream, bear right onto Wassataquoik Stream Trail.

Wassataquoik Lake from
the day-use beach

The stream will be your constant companion until you reach the main stem of Wassataquoik Stream. As you hike along, the trail crosses several small streams. You get occasional views of the surrounding mountains—a view of the graveled face of North Turner Mountain and the hump of Caverly Lookout. By the time the stream widens before joining with Wassataquoik Stream, you'll have glimpsed all the surrounding mountains.

The ford of Wassataquoik Stream is at a wide, shallow spot above a large pool. The streambed is rounded wash stones that offer easy footing. Across the stream, the trail goes between Wassataquoik Stream and Turner Brook, mostly out of sight of both. You pass through the site of New City.

Russell Pond campground is strung out along the south and west shore of the pond. The rental canoes, bunkhouse, information kiosk, and several lean-tos are where Russell Pond Trail ends at the pond. The ranger's station and spring are along the Grand Falls Trail on the north side Russell Pond.

A short walk through the campground on Pogy Notch Trail brings you to Wassataquoik Lake Trail. Follow this trail west. It climbs gently to the side trail to Deep Pond. There's no view from the shore, but if you take the canoe across the pond you'll have fine views of the mountains to the south. Also, explore the bog at the east end of the pond.

Grand Falls

Continuing on Wassataquoik Lake Trail, you enter Six Ponds Basin. The trail crosses an esker between the ponds. At a break in the esker is access to a pond on each side of the trail. There are rental canoes. Watch for ducks in the ponds.

The trail continues to Wassataquoik Lake. Past the side trail to Wassataquoik Island lean-to—yes, the lean-to is on an island you must canoe to—the trail comes to the shore of the lake. You have a fine view down the length of the long, narrow body of water squeezed between South Pogy and Wassataquoik Mountains. Cliffs drop into the water on both shores, mostly toward the far end of the lake.

From the lake shore, the trail turns inland to loop around a large, moldering mass of granite before reaching the day-use area. There's a canoe and a small gravel and bedrock beach.

The trail continues along Wassataquoik Lake to Green Falls before climbing to Little Wassataquoik, where there's a tent site and a side trail to the top of a granite dome overlooking the lake.

Grand Falls Trail starts at the northwest corner of Russell Pond. The trail passes the ranger's station—there's a fine view from the dock—and the short trail to the spring. Along the shore of Russell Pond is a big blueberry patch. In fact, the trails in the Wassataquoik Valley are often lined with blueberries.

The trail climbs away from the pond up a rocky slope. The Caverly Lookout Trail angles northeast, climbing steadily through a mixed forest. As you climb, the ridge

Russell Mountain and Katahdin from the blueberry patch next to the Russell Pond ranger's station

narrows and partial views open up. The trail ends at a large boulder on the ridge's high point. Step south around the boulder to a dome of granite with fine views south and west. This viewpoint is named for Buzz Caverly who was a Baxter ranger for forty years, ending as director until his retirement in 2005.

Back on the Grand Falls Trail, you skirt around Caverly Overlook's steep slopes. After a short descent, the trail reaches Bell Pond. The north shore of the pond is a jumble of angular boulders and scratchy greenery. From the shore, you have fine views of the mountains to the south. Watch for ducks and moose in the pond.

Bell Pond is shaped like an elongated hourglass. Its east end is a good-sized bog. Where the trail crosses the bog, look for carnivorous plants growing in the dense moss. The trail then crosses a low, rocky knoll along Bell Pond's outlet. From the knoll, you can see Wassataquoik Stream.

The trail reaches a junction. All three trails are called Grand Falls Trail. Turn left, following the shore of Wassataquoik Stream. It's a short walk to Grand Falls. In Maine, traditionally "falls" are steep rapids and "pitches" are waterfalls. Most rivers have a Grand Falls and/or a grand pitch. Here on the Wassataquoik Stream, Grand Falls is a quarter-mile section of steep water that pours through a narrow, granite gorge dropping 100 feet. The stream drops in a series of small falls and fights through boulder fields. The trail skirts the top of cliffs overlooking this maelstrom.

Ledge Falls

It's possible, with great care, to climb down into the gorge near the end of the trail to a good swimming hole. Just downstream, beyond the end of the trail, is the site of Old City. Like New City, all that's left is a collection of fields being reclaimed by forest. A sluggish Wassataquoik Stream empties into the East Branch 15 miles below Grand Falls. The only evidence of its upstream energy is a long gravel bar that reaches well upstream from the confluence.

Just west of the three-way junction, the trail crosses Bell Pond's outlet, where it empties into Wassataquoik Stream. Inscription Rock is the huge boulder sitting on the edge of the stream. The inscription is mostly worn off, visible now as a stain on the face of the boulder.

The next half mile of the trail, where it passes between Wassataquoik Stream and Bell Pond, is overgrown and beaver-flooded. With care, you can find your way without getting wet. You get a nice view of Caverly Lookout from the open woods south of Bell Pond.

There's no access to Ledge Falls. When the trail passes beside the falls, find a likely place and force your way through the underbrush onto one of the ledges. Wassataquoik Stream slides over a series of wide granite ledges. From the ledges, you can look downstream and see The Traveler framed by the woods. Above and below Ledge Falls are pools for swimming or washing off a day's grime.

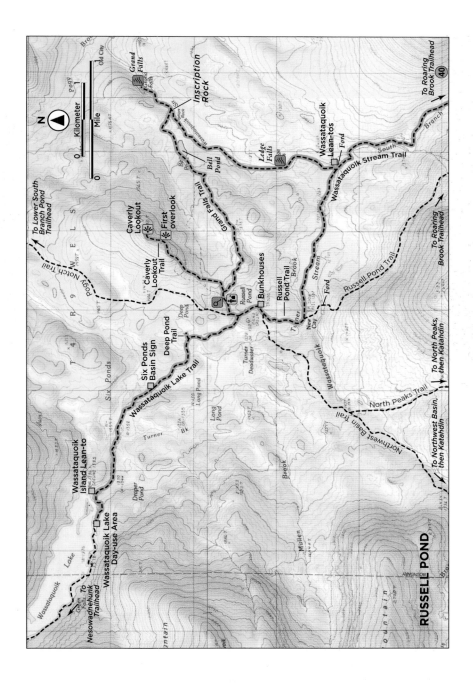

N

Kilometer 0 1

Mile 0 1

Old City

Pogy Brook

Grand Falls

Inscription Rock

Grand Falls Trail

Bell Pond

Ledge Falls

Wassataquoik Lean-tos

Ford

Wassataquoik Stream Trail

To Roaring Brook Trailhead 40

To Roaring Brook Trailhead

To Lower South Branch Pond Trailhead

Pogy Notch Trail

Caverly Lookout

First overlook

Caverly Lookout Trail

Deep Pond Trail

Bunkhouses

Russell Pond

Russell Pond Trail

Turner Brook

Stream

Ford

New City

Russell Pond Trail

Wassataquoik

Six Ponds Basin Sign

Six Ponds

Wassataquoik Lake Trail

Deep Pond

Turner Deadwater

Long Pond

Long Pond

Turner

North Peaks Trail

To North Peaks, then Katahdin

Northwest Basin Trail

To Northwest Basin, then Katahdin

Wassataquoik Island Lean-to

Wassataquoik Lake Day-use Area

Draper Pond

Green Falls To Nesowadnehunk Trailhead

Wassataquoik Lake

Mullen Brook

Brook

ountain

RUSSELL POND

A short distance beyond Ledge Falls, Grand Falls Trail ends at Wassataquoik Stream Trail near the river ford. It's an easy, level walk back to Russell Pond.

For this hike, you return from Russell Pond to Roaring Brook Trailhead following Russell Pond Trail the whole way. If you are more adventurous or can arrange a shuttle, consider returning via another route such as Pogy Notch Trail.

Backcountry camping fees and permit required. Non–Maine residents also pay an auto entrance fee.

MILES AND DIRECTIONS

DAY 1

0.0 Start from the Roaring Brook Trailhead at the north end of the day-use parking area.

0.1 In 350 feet, pass the ranger's station and then Chimney Pond Trail. Go straight onto the Russell Pond Trail, crossing the bridge over Roaring Brook. Pass Roaring Brook Nature Trail and then Sandy Stream Pond Trail.

1.2 Pass the north end of Sandy Stream Pond Trail.

1.4 A short bog boardwalk leads to the shore of Whidden Pond.

2.7 The trail passes a very large boulder.

3.3 The trail approaches South Branch of Wassataquoik Stream. Bear right onto the Wassataquoik Stream Trail.

5.7 The trail crosses numerous small brooks. Pass the short side trail to Wassataquoik Stream lean-tos. The trail turns left and crosses a small channel of the stream to an island.

5.8 Cross the island along the shore of Wassataquoik Stream to the ford.

5.9 Ford the stream. In summer, the water is usually about knee deep with moderate current. In spring, this crossing can be dangerous. Across the stream, reenter the woods and turn left at the junction, staying on the Wassataquoik Stream Trail.

6.5 The trail crosses relatively level ground between Turner Brook and Wassataquoik Stream, passing through the site of New City.

7.3 Turn right onto Russell Pond Trail and immediately cross Turner Brook below a beaver dam.

7.7 Pass Northwest Basin Trail.

7.8 Reach Russell Pond campground along the south and west shore of Russell Pond.

DAY 2

0.0 From the junction of Russell Pond and Pogy Notch Trails hike north through the campground.

0.2 Turn left onto Wassataquoik Lake Trail.

0.6   Turn right onto Deep Pond Trail.

0.7   Reach Deep Pond. There's a rental canoe. To continue the hike, return to Wassataquoik Lake Trail.

0.8   Turn right onto Wassataquoik Lake Trail.

1.4   The trail passes a no-longer-maintained trail. There's a sign noting that you've reached Six Ponds Basin.

1.8   The trail crosses and esker to Six Ponds where two pond almost meet. There's a rental canoe.

2.3   Cross Turner Brook.

2.4   Pass Wassataquoik Island Lean-to Trail.

2.5   The trail descends to the southeast end of the lake.

2.7   The trail turns away from the lake and climbs around a granite knob. Turn right onto the day-use area trail.

2.8   Reach the south shore of Wassataquoik Lake. There's a rental canoe and a small gravel and bedrock beach. To complete the hike, return the way you came to Russell Pond. OPTIONS: Green Falls is another 0.9 mile west on Wassataquoik Lake Trail. Wassataquoik Lookout is 2.5 miles west on Wassataquoik Lake Trail.

5.3   Arrive back at Russell Pond campground.

DAY 3

0.0   From the junction of Russell Pond and Pogy Notch Trails hike north through the campground.

0.2   Turn right onto Grand Falls Trail.

0.3   Pass the ranger's station on the right along the north shore of Russell Pond. Just past the ranger's station, a side trail leads away from the pond to a spring.

0.5   Climb away from Russell Pond and turn left onto Caverly Lookout Trail.

1.2   Climb steadily to the first overlook.

1.4   The trail ends at Caverly Lookout. To continue the hike, return the way you came to Grand Falls Trail.

2.3   Turn left onto Grand Falls Trail.

3.7   Reach the north shore of Bell Pond.

4.0   The trail passes Bell Pond, then crosses a boardwalk across a bog.

4.1   Turn left toward Grand Falls just before Wassataquoik Stream.

4.5   The trail follows the top of the gorge with numerous overlooks at the falls. The trail ends at the base of the falls atop a cliff. To continue the hike, return to the last junction.

4.9   Bear left at the junction toward Wassataquoik Stream.

5.0   The trail crosses Bell Pond's outlet and passes Inscription Rock.

5.2   The trail crosses an overgrown and flooded section south of Bell Pond.

5.7 Cross a small brook below a beaver dam.

6.1 Reach Ledge Falls. There's no viewpoint or access to Wassataquoik Stream. You need to force your way through the underbrush to reach the ledges.

6.8 Grand Falls Trail ends at Wassataquoik Stream Trail near the ford. Go straight on Wassataquoik Stream Trail (retracing your arrival at Russell Pond two days ago).

8.0 Turn right onto Russell Pond Trail and cross Turner Brook.

8.7 Arrive back at Russell Pond campground.

DAY 4

0.0 From Russell Pond campground, follow Russell Pond Trail south.

0.1 Pass Northwest Basin Trail.

0.5 Cross Turner Brook and pass Wassataquoik Stream Trail.

0.7 Ford Wassataquoik Stream. This crossing is rocky and uneven. It can be dangerous in spring or other high-water times.

2.3 Climb away from Wassataquoik Stream and slab around Russell Mountain, crossing a good-sized stream.

3.7 Pass through an interesting boulder field and descend to cross South Branch Wassataquoik Stream.

3.9 Pass the south end of Wassataquoik Stream Trail.

7.3 Arrive back at the trailhead.

TRAIL FINDER

Best Hikes for Swimming

4. Middle Fowler Pond
6. South Branch Falls
7. Howe Brook Falls
20. Lily Pad Pond
21. Niagara Falls
28. Little Abol Falls
29. Blueberry Ledges
39. Katahdin Lake
40. Russell Pond

Best Hikes for Views

2. Trout Brook Mountain
5. Barrell Ridge
8. The Traveler
9. Black Cat Mountain
10. Burnt Mountain
12. Doubletop Mountain
13. North Brother
14. Mount Coe
15. Mount O-J-I
19. Sentinel Mountain
20. Lily Pad Pond
25. The Owl
26. Katahdin via the Hunt Trail
27. Katahdin via Abol Trail
33. South Turner Mountain
34. North Peaks
35. North Basin
36. Katahdin via The Knife Edge
38. Northwest Basin
39. Katahdin Lake
40. Russell Pond

Best Hikes for Waterfalls

4. Middle Fowler Pond
6. South Branch Falls
7. Howe Brook Falls
20. Lily Pad Pond
21. Niagara Falls
25. The Owl
26. Katahdin via the Hunt Trail
28. Little Abol Falls
29. Blueberry Ledges
40. Russell Pond

Best Hikes for Blueberries

5. Barrell Ridge
8. The Traveler
19. Sentinel Mountain
23. Foss & Knowlton Pond
24. Grassy Pond Loop
29. Blueberry Ledges
32. Rum Pond
35. North Basin
40. Russell Pond

Best Hike for Geology

3. Five Ponds Loop
6. South Branch Falls
8. The Traveler
12. Doubletop Mountain
13. North Brother
14. Mount Coe
15. Mount O-J-I
21. Niagara Falls
26. Katahdin via the Hunt Trail
27. Katahdin via Abol Trail
29. Blueberry Ledges
30. Kettle Pond